MW01288904

Make Way For The Lady Ensign

An American Memoir

by

Kay Thompson Baxter

PAX AMERICANA
PRODUCTIONS

In 1991, Kay Thompson Baxter's adult children asked her to write her memoir. They wanted to know more about their mother's life growing up on a farm in the Piedmont region of North Carolina and her experiences as a United States Navy Nurse during World War II. Twenty-five years later, her book remains an eloquent personal history.

This powerful, slim volume offers important insights into the military servicewomen of America's Greatest Generation. Educational, funny, and poignant, *MAKE WAY FOR THE LADY ENSIGN: An American Memoir* is the autobiography of a gracious and courageous woman.

Sally M. Tibbetts
A Bookworm in Cyber Space

To every thing there is a season, and a time to every purpose under heaven:

A time to be born, and a time to die; a time to plant, and a time to pluck up that which is planted;

A time to kill, and a time to heal; a time to break down, and a time to laugh; a time to mourn, and a time to dance;

A time to cast away stones, and a time to gather stones together; a time to embrace, and a time to refrain from embracing;

A time to get, and a time to lose; a time to keep, and a time to cast away;

A time to rend, and a time to sew; a time to keep silence, and a time to speak;

A time to love, and a time to hate;

A time of war, and a time of peace.

Ecclesiastes 3:1-8

Copyright © Kay Thompson Baxter

Cataloging-in-Publication Data is on file at the Library of Congress

ISBN-13: 978-1532964633
ISBN-10: 1532964633

Published by Pax Americana Productions, LLC.

Make Way For The Lady Ensign: An American Memoir

FIRST EDITION 2016

Book design by Fran Strauss

Printed in the United States of America

Official Facebook Page:
Make Way For The Lady Ensign: An American Memoir

FOREWORD

For the past few years, my two children have expressed their wishes for a written account of my life. Barbara tells me that my grandchildren would enjoy reading about it. Billy Jr. informed me that I could leave out the X-rated version, if I'd like. He said he wanted to read the stories about my childhood on the farm – its smells, descriptions, how I felt, what clothes I wore. Barbara and Billy wanted to have a record of my experiences as a United States Navy Nurse during World War II – where, who, and how I felt as a woman among so many men.

Well, my own dear children, this is for you. It won't tell all, but it will be true and as accurate as my memory permits. Please remember as you read that I am reliving and writing just as events occur to me, and my feelings are expressed as I felt then and remember now.

You have enriched my life beyond measure, and I love you without reservations of any kind. It is rewarding to know a small part of me will live on in you and your children.

Mom
April 30, 1991

1.   BUCKETS OF COLD WATER

I was born August 8, 1915, a sunny and hot Sunday morning. My father, John William Thompson, was a farmer in the Piedmont region of North Carolina. My mother, Katherine Neely Fleming, grew up across the road from his home. Although they celebrated the same birthday, Dad was ten years older. Word is he was a popular young man with the local ladies and did not particularly notice Mother until her sixteenth birthday. They married in 1905 when she turned eighteen.

I was the third child born in our family. My brother Earl was six years older than I and my sister Mary Wood four years older. There were two younger brothers, J.W. Jr. (Jay) and Paul, who were respectively two and four years younger than I.

My earliest memory is of being cradled in Dad's arms. We were in our yard and Mother and Mary Wood were standing beside us. My sister tells me that when she would take a toy from me or refuse to give me something I wanted, I would hold my breath till I fainted. That is her recollection. I cannot refute it.

I also have dim mental pictures of riding in a surrey while Mother brushed my hair and tied a fancy sash around my dress. Our transportation was by buggy or surrey, which were much alike save for size and passenger room. Both had black canvas covers for protection from the weather and were pulled by horses. The buggy was smaller, had but one horse, and the top cover could be folded down so we would have more freedom on the warm and sunny days.

When we traveled as a family we used the surrey. It was a full two-seater carriage with kerosene lamps on the front sides and fringes around the top. The sides could be either opened or closed, but the top was permanently fixed – like a roof. Two horses, sometimes at a brisk pace, drove this vehicle. If you have seen the Broadway Musical "Oklahoma" you may remember the lyrics: "The surrey with the fringe on top" – this was it.

I remember being dressed by Mother while she held me close to her tummy, which was very big. I learned my brown locks were difficult for her to keep neat, so she was taking me to the photography studio for a last picture before cutting those curls. This was right before brother Paul was born.

In all large families children divide into groups. Mary Wood and Earl were always together and my two younger brothers Jay and Paul romped about like puppies, playing and wrestling. I did not have a playmate. I entertained myself with make-believe stories and lived in my fantasy world. My siblings could get me to do almost anything by promising to tell me a story. Although there were few toys in our home, I had a rag doll to talk with and love. And little kittens became my friends too.

The driveway at home was about half a mile straight to Highway 70 with the Southern Railroad tracks running across it near to the junction. One time, Earl and Mary Wood and I ran to the tracks and waved to the men in uniforms who filled several cars of a train. They were the last of the returning Doughboys from World War I.

Our house was a large two-story white wooden building set well back from the highway. The driveway led straight through our yard and then curved left toward an immense oak tree. Our yard was large enough but not unusually so. Dad hated to waste any of his cropland.

Several steps led to the front porch, which wrapped partially around two sides of our house. At the right hand corner was a swing, everyone's favorite spot on hot summer days and evenings. A settee (small slatted bench) and two wicker chairs completed the porch furniture.

Inside the front door was a wide hallway with a door on the right leading to the master bedroom; the left door to the parlor. Along the right wall, an old-fashioned hall tree – a tall-mirrored piece of furniture with large hooks for coats and hats. Hung on the wall beyond it, a huge map of Jerusalem and Solomon's Temple: Dad's Masonic Lodge Chart.

To the left was the stairway to the second floor that had

a smaller hallway with three bedrooms opening from it. Mary Wood and I shared one room, the center room was a guest room, and the largest room belonged to my three brothers. We children slept on iron beds but the guest room had nice oak furniture. Of course under all beds were the chamber pots, the one in our guest room matching a large pitcher and washbowl set atop a stand.

Our parlor had a small potbelly stove. The master bedroom and dining room had fireplaces with mantels over them. The kitchen included a black iron wood-burning stove, a large rectangular table with straight wicker bottom chairs around it, and an antique pie safe. Later, there was some extensive remodeling to make an entire wall of cabinets.

Our back porch was entirely screened with doors leading to it from the back hallway, dining room, and kitchen. Inside the shed attached to the far back door was a porcelain bathtub that was not hooked up to any water supply, only a sort of trough filled with cold water and big crockery jars containing milk and butter.

In our back yard was a giant tank filled with carbide crystals for a special type of electricity. I was warned it was dangerous and stayed away from that area. There was also a chopping block into which an axe was usually stuck. Dad chopped the wood for the fireplaces and stoves.

Nearby was the smokehouse containing hams and other cured meats and barrels of pickles and sauerkraut. This building was kept locked. Attached to it was our woodshed loaded with Dad's chopping efforts.

In back of the smokehouse were three galvanized tubs placed on a bench. Not far away, a big iron pot hanging over a pile of ashes which was cold except on washdays. This was our laundry area. Dirty clothes were boiled in a pot of water and soap powder, and then scrubbed in one of the tubs by using a washboard. Often our Aunt Choll, a black woman, did this work. She received the going rate of thirty-five to fifty cents a day for her labor.

The woodshed was on the edge of our orchard, lined with plum and damson trees on the right side. Along those trees a path led to the outhouse, a place I feared entering alone. I once came upon a snake on the path leading to it and found the outhouse very dark when I shut the door. Often I waited and waited, hoping for Mother or Mary Wood to accompany me there.

Most of the trees in our orchard bore peaches; we also had a few apples and pear trees. When the spring blossoms arrived it was a fragrant and beautiful spot for daydreaming.

Hen houses were located at the end of the orchard near the barn. There were many chambers for chickens and nests for their eggs. In addition to bringing firewood into the house, I had chores with the chicks. I gathered eggs into a basket and scattered feed as directed by Mother.

Just beyond the large oak tree at the end of the driveway was a corncrib and an open shed for our tractor, plows, and other farm equipment.

In close proximity was a large two-story barn. Under the first part of it was storage space for the surrey, buggy, and the big wagon. There were stalls for horses and mules, and on the opposite side were stables for the half dozen or so cows. Topside we stored hay that was tossed downward to feed the livestock.

Bales of hay and straw were stacked outside the barn. I would take visiting cousins there to play, but Dad chased us away saying it was no play area. I have heard about other farm children having great fun in barn lofts and on haystacks, but Dad was adamant about that.

Back of the barn was a barnyard that the cows and horses shared. Behind this were the pigpens where swine rooted for food and drink, wallowing in the mud grunting and squealing. It smelled bad regardless of anyone's efforts.

I hated that place.

A path led from the barn area through the woods and down across a brook and then up a hill. There were many dogwood trees in those woods that were especially lovely at springtime. The top of the hill was my favorite spot, but I never went there alone for it seemed too far from our house.

Two miles away was the local school, a wooden

building that had two classrooms and grass yard in front. Around back there was a shed for horses and buggies. During my first year, we kept Uncle Baxter's Shetland Pony back there, which my older brother Earl hitched to our buggy for rides to and from school.

In my classroom were the first three grades. Teacher separated us into groups and assigned tasks to two groups while instructing a third one. I listened to everything the teaching group was reading, saying, and doing. It was fascinating and I learned a bit too.

After two years in the small schoolhouse, we transferred to a bigger school with one teacher to each grade in Cleveland, North Carolina. That was probably a mistake because the school and its students were new to me, I was a bit shy, younger than anyone in my class, and I was absolutely lost with the math lessons. The third graders now called me Teacher's Pet. The fourth graders were not friendly either.

Recess was not much fun that year.

In the early 1920s, we bought a touring car that had to be hand-cranked from the front. Its top could be lowered in the warmer months. Earl was permitted to drive us to school in the car. Our horse drawn vehicles became passé.

I checked-out books from the library and began reading every moment I could steal away from my chores. I hid books in the woodpile so I could sit down out there and escape anyone who wanted to keep me busy. My sister would call out for help with the dishes (she washed, I dried). I'd just yell back, "Yes!" and keep reading. Although Earl was a high school senior and I a sixth grader, I'd borrow his history and geography books. It angered him no end that I enjoyed his books more than he did.

I once sassed my sixth grade teacher in front of the entire class. She and I really were fond of each other. But on that day she kept me after school, she talked with me, she cried, and then she switched my legs. I then cried. But mostly because Dad said if we were punished at school, he would punish us again when we got home. I did get punished on schedule. I was so embarrassed I doubled my efforts that spring and ended up with a prize for the best sixth grade book reports in Rowan County.

Time passed and changes occurred on the farm. Electric lines ran out from the city. We had lights and a refrigerator instead of the old icebox. A complete bathroom was added to the house with tub, sink, and commode. There were sinks in the kitchen and on the back porch. Instead of the hand pump we had another well dug and an electric pump meter was installed. There were even lights and running water inside the barn.

Mother tried to teach me how to milk cows but I just could not get any milk into the bucket. Perhaps I did not try very hard. I was excused from that futile exercise and was given extra work cleaning the chicken coops. I might have fared better with the cows.

We females did not do the hard fieldwork, however, we spent long hours hoeing cotton and corn and doing the necessary work in our vegetable garden. We gathered fruits from the orchard and grapes from the arbor. We picked wild strawberries in spring and blackberries in summer. Doing these jobs we wore our brothers' coveralls and either wide-brim bonnets or straw hats.

Mother canned vegetables and fruits for winter use and I had to peel and cut lots of peaches. Most luscious ones never made it to the canning stage. I ate them until I was sated. And peaches are still my favorite fruit.

In the fall there were fields of cotton to be picked by hand. We never skipped classes for farm work, but we did rush to the cotton patch immediately upon arriving home from school. We worked from sunup to dusk on Saturdays. Never on a Sunday. Sacks were tied around our waists, the size of the sacks depending upon our age and strength. It was hard on our hands because cotton bolls have sharp points encasing the white fluff center that we then pulled out and put into our sacks. The chief reason we were industrious was because our loads were weighed – we were paid one cent for each pound we picked.

Fluffy cotton weighs very little.

Most of our crop was wheat, which is harvested in

the middle of the summer. Dad and my brothers ran the tractor and reaper. Later on we had a combine that made work easier.

Then came the threshers.

Dad hired a crew of men and a big threshing machine. A few black men were paid and our neighbors always helped. We would return their assistance in time. There were always more than a dozen extra mouths to feed for a few days each summer. Mother and Aunt Lou would bake and prepare food for days. I have counted eight to ten fruit pies cooling on a cupboard counter. I took buckets of cold water to the workingmen and served them food. We had a table in the dining room and another on the back porch, and there would still be a second sitting of hungry field hands.

I enjoyed the excitement of the annual threshing.

For a few weeks there would be almost a vacation time after the summer wheat harvest. We would make homemade ice cream and invite friends to share it. I remember a beach trip with my mother and Uncle Joe and Earl and Paul. Because the farm animals required everyday attention, my father and Mary Wood and Jay stayed home. Then perhaps the next year the order might be reversed. At least, Dad saw to it that Mother got away.

Farm life was pleasant, but nothing as exciting as my romantic fantasies.

2. A BEST FRIEND WITH A COUSIN

Bus service started for us at the beginning of Earl's senior year. He drove our bus and I had the job of keeping it clean. Earl went away to college and Mary Wood followed the next year. Earl planned to be a Presbyterian minister and Mary Wood a teacher.

Along came the stock market crash of 1929 and the Great Depression.

Money became scarce and Dad worried about the mortgage on our farm. Some years earlier two salesman from Paul Rubber Company had convinced him to invest so he could send his children to college. Dad mortgaged the farm and now his investment had disappeared. We always had plenty of good food but not much money for extras.

Now we cutback even more.

I graduated from high school at fifteen. Although I had been to parties I never had a "real" date with a boy. Occasionally, a classmate asked for my help with his homework, but that was only being a best friend with a cousin.

Graduation night we sat on the stage. Our senior class had twenty-one students, ten boys and eleven girls. That night only ten girls were in our graduating group. The boys had failed the grammar and writing tests.

Ruby, the prettiest and best-dressed girl in the class, was salutatorian. When she got up to welcome the audience she said, "We welcome you." Ruby stopped and repeated those same words a time or two then sat down. After the main speaker's address I was to deliver the valedictory. I looked out at the audience. I saw my mother, father, and my two younger brothers. Paul was very serious, pale, leaning intently over the seat in front of him and looking straight at me. On our way home he said, "Catherine, I just trembled for you."

My youngest brother's statement is still one of the

most heartwarming things ever said to me.

It was time for college. And I was eager to go. I felt life would really begin if I could only go to some wonderful school far away from the farm. Although I loved my home and family, I was sure greater things were out there. Reading my Sunday school literature about faraway places, I thought I'd like to be a missionary just for the travel. I was offered partial scholarships at two colleges, however, Mother finally told me it would be too much for Dad to handle. My older brother and sister were still in college.

I spent 1931 raising hundreds of little chicks to make a bit of money, taught a Sunday school class, started a Young People's Group at church, and continued reading hours each day.

When the fall of 1932 arrived, I received an education loan from the synod of our church and I applied for a waitress position in the Mitchell College dining room. That job included setting tables and running the electric dishwasher. Mother bought me a few outfits. And there I was, not exactly where I wanted to be, but finally in college.

Mitchell College in Statesville was founded in 1852 as a two-story female seminary. In 1932 it was still a Presbyterian junior college. That year, male day students were admitted for the first time. The building was pure Greek architecture, having six large columns in the front. It was now three stories tall and covered by wisteria vines. In addition to college students, there were a few junior and senior high schoolers and about thirty commercial students at Mitchell. The total student body was around two hundred.

My main interest continued to be my studies. I just could not bear to think anyone should get better grades than I did. I made a few good friends especially among the group who worked with me in the dining hall.

I had a boyfriend before Christmas. Whit was the young music professor at Mitchell. Perhaps he enjoyed my family and the farm. We sat on the front porch swing in the moonlight reading poetry; and he played our piano for hours. We were together only on weekends at my home, but it seemed so romantic.

For Christmas, Whit cut varying lengths of metal pipes and strung them in our hallway. He played them as chimes. We took Jay and Paul with us on a mountain trip, climbing Grandfather Mountain through the snow and returning the same night.

Whit had graduated from Yale and spent fourteen months in Europe. That impressed me greatly. In the early spring of my second year, I looked at my friends and their dates and decided I was not having nearly as much fun as they were having with boys our own age. My relationship with Whit was totally innocent. I had remained young for my age, naïve, without the vaguest idea of my own sexuality.

That spring I had a few dates with one of the young men in the college choir, but all school dates were dull occasions. We only had permission to sit in the main parlor from eight until ten in the evenings while our dean of students, a strict elderly lady, walked in circles watching to see if we sat too close. Very few fellows returned after those dates.

May of 1934, I graduated from Mitchell with sixty-four college credits and a Class C Teacher's Certificate. I won the English and Bible medals, was May Queen, and Valedictorian. Our family financial situation again precluded more college education. And despite my good record, I was neither confident nor aggressive enough to get a teaching position.

Fall of 1934, I decided to get into something else.

Mary Wood, who was teaching, suggested nursing school was inexpensive and would be a good career. I began to like the idea, wrote for information, and visited a couple of places. In February 1935, I enrolled at the Watts School of Nursing in Durham, North Carolina.

Watts Hospital was made up of groups of stucco buildings roofed with orange-red tiles and surrounded by lovely green lawns. There were separate quarters for nurses, and the main building had long connecting corridors to three wings. This place had an open sunny look since one wall of the corridors was all glass. Watts felt more pleasant and homelike than I had imagined a hospital to be.

At last I was the same age as my classmates and I was comfortable in my group. Agatha was my best friend and roommate. We were more intense and studious than most, but we enjoyed good times with our other friends.

Probationary period lasted six months. Then we started working two hours a day at the hospital, gradually increasing the time until we might even work eight hours on the weekends. This was in addition to classroom hours and the practical demonstrations of nursing procedures.

A month into my probationary term, my instructor found me leaning weakly against a door. She grabbed a wheelchair, took my temperature, pulse, respirations, and rushed me to a bed in one of the hospital's private wings. My temperature was over 104° and I was barely coherent, vaguely aware of a needle in my arm and a bottle hanging on a pole by my bed. Doctors were in and out thumping my chest and taking x-rays. I was lethargic and my temperature remained elevated for days. There were cooling baths, poultices, and steam inhalations. I could not hold down any liquids. I was told I had pleurisy.

Then one day, I awakened to find Mother and Dad by my bed. They had been called and rushed to see me. I believe their concern was a turning point. When they came to visit me again the next morning, I was alert. My supervisor wanted me to go home and recover until the next classes started. I argued that I could catch up with all that I had missed. Mother and Dad backed me up.
Ten days later, I returned to school. The studies were no problem, but it did take some time for me to catch up with some of the practical procedures I missed.

By the second year, we were on night duty from eleven pm. to seven am. The night supervisor checked us carefully, made frequent rounds, and came promptly when called. I had four weeks of duty with no nights off. And on Tuesdays, I had classes almost every other hour until four p.m. But, I survived it. And I began to feel I was becoming a nurse.

There were occasional parties in our lounge, and I

had a few dates with University of North Carolina students from Chapel Hill who had been my patients. But my main goal was still my career preparation.

Operating Room Duty was a demanding assignment at first. We awoke at five a.m. to prepare for early surgery. It was necessary to surgically scrub, don sterile gear, and setup tables for the operations scheduled for the day. Some operations were long and tedious affairs and at times the surgeons were quite rude.

At the end of each and every day we cleaned, scoured the bloody instruments, repacked surgical tools and sets of special linens for specific operations, and autoclaved everything. There were hundreds of gloves to be washed, powdered, and packaged before sterilization. Once or twice, I got up at five a.m. and never saw my room again until two or three a.m. the next morning. When it became too much for me, I asked for a weekend back home.

Seeing my family again restored my balance and confidence. When I returned to Watts, I enjoyed the operating room. I became instrument nurse for the most demanding surgeon there. One day, he turned to me after a particularly difficult operation and said, "Thank you, sister."

I felt like a winner.

Three years passed and it was graduation day and then time for state boards. All North Carolina graduating nurses went to Raleigh for three days of written and oral exams and for procedure demonstrations.

After our last exam, someone bought a bottle of Virginia Dare wine and I had my first alcoholic drink. We bought more and I drank more. Then I became tearful, saying I had failed the exams. My good friend Stewie put me in the shower and I told her, "I am in Venice riding in a gondola."

Two weeks later, I was handed the Durham Herald Sun with my yearbook photograph and a story headline on the front page:

WATTS NURSE LEADS GIRLS TAKING EXAM

I did it. I made the highest test scores in North Carolina.

Months prior to graduating, acting upon the suggestion of our Director of Nurses, I had applied to Teacher's College at Columbia University in New York City for admission to their degree program. I was accepted with a minimal scholarship and reserved a room for September 1938 admission. If all went well, twelve months later I would have my Bachelor of Science in Nursing (BSN).

Life did not go as I planned.

During a brief visit home Mother talked with me about Dad's failing health, the tight family budget, their concern for fairness to each child, and my father's love and devotion regarding me and my future. I realized for years Mother and Dad had the very best loving relationship. It was always evident in their actions – that gentle touch, a look, the caring between them. Whenever my father punished, he said it was because he loved us, and to teach us right from wrong. He was truly proud of his family, telling friends about his children and our small successes. Mother made me understand it would be selfish to accept more financial help when I could ease their burden by taking care of myself.

The new Director of Nurses gave me a position of head nurse on the private maternity ward. My duties included women in labor, their post-partum care, and supervision of the nursery for their newborn babies. It was a satisfying job even though the salary was only fifty dollars per month plus room and board.

I now lived in the staff house across the street with many of my classmates. We became friends with a great group of young men in Durham. Several times a week, we got together and went to movies or some small café to dance and have a beer. We were really and truly good friends with no pairing off. When one of us could not go out, another friend took his or her place and there were no possessive or jealous scenes. We were sort of next-door neighbor friends.

In 1940, we received letters from the Red Cross asking for volunteers to join the Navy or Army Reserve

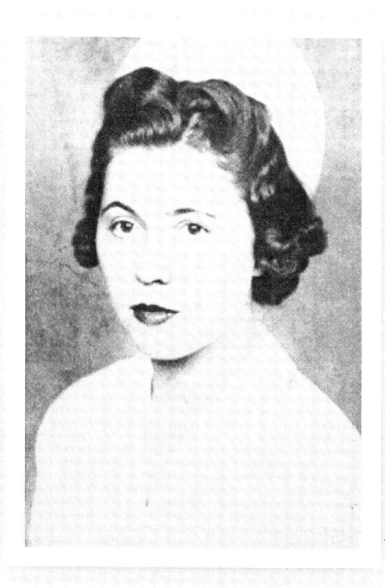

Nurse Corps. Three of us signed up for the Navy and had interviews and physicals, never dreaming we would leave Durham. But in the early spring of 1941, Nell, Stewie, and I received letters from the Navy Department giving us the opportunity to accept a year's active duty at the U.S. Naval Hospital in Charleston, South Carolina. We decided it could be a great adventure. I left North Carolina on May 20, 1941, and they were to follow me in a few weeks.

No sad goodbyes for me. I wanted adventure.

3. THE GRACEFUL SLIDE OF SHIPS INTO THE SEA

After arriving by taxi at the gate of Charleston Naval Yard, I was directed to a group of white buildings some distance away. A rather short, older nurse greeted me. "Miss Thompson, why have you brought a trunk here?" she asked me.

"I planned to leave it at the nurses' residence."

"There is no residence as of yet," she explained. "You will have to make other arrangements."

She telephoned the local YWCA for a room and sent me back ten miles into the city via Navy transportation.

I knew now I was an adult and needed to learn self-reliance. I wrote my roommates and told them I believed I'd be paying Uncle Sam for the privilege of working for him.

The following day, I was kept busy as I began to learn about Navy paperwork. There seemed to be seven copies for everything I signed. So many of the Navy regulations, I could hardly imagine what they were about. I was measured for a regular Navy nurse uniform, and I was horrified to find the dress length near my ankles. But I kept quiet. I also learned I would receive extra pay for food and lodging. Then I noticed some small print above my signature and found I'd just signed the following:

I understand that I am in the United States Navy for a least one (1) year and/or the duration of the Emergency.

A few days later President Roosevelt signed a Proclamation of National Emergency.

There were only five nurses, all older than I. The wards were jammed with sailors performing tasks. When I inquired about them, I was told most of them were patients assigned to light duties awaiting orders.

Miss Dean, the chief nurse, knew I wanted to find an

apartment for Nell, Stewie, and myself and asked another nurse to drive me and make sure I found a place south of Broad Street.

I found the ideal spot at 9 Church Street just off South Battery in the Old Hastie House, a National Landmark, owned at that time by Doctor and Mrs. Jervey Ravenel. The side of the house adjacent to the street had a wrought iron gate. The front of the house had long balconies overlooking the battery at the junction of the Cooper and Ashley rivers.

The Ravenels rented me two large third-floor bedrooms with a connecting bath. Both rooms had doors opening onto the balcony. I moved in immediately and wrote to my friends about our wonderful new home. Upon their arrival, we also rented a third room across the wide hallway and that room became a combination living room, dining room, and kitchen. Our kitchen was really only a two-burner hot plate, atop a shelf in a large closet with a window inside it. We did prepare some good meals. Friends soon found our apartment a congenial place to visit. The Ravenels were a gracious couple and we enjoyed life there.

S.O.Q. (Sick Officers Quarters) was my first assignment. No one seemed very ill and it was a friendly atmosphere. One of my patients, an ensign awaiting orders to his ship, invited me to the Pink Coat, a cocktail lounge overlooking the water at the Fort Sumter Hotel. He suggested a daiquiri and I thought that quite sophisticated. My escort was handsome, gallant, an officer and a gentleman.

Many ships were in port and the officers were eager for companionship. Miss Dean turned out to be a true friend. She told the three of us she was especially happy we were enjoying an active social life. She threw a cocktail party at her garden apartment. And once took a group of us to a lovely and gracious restaurant, the Brewton Inn.

There were so many places to go in Charleston. Folly Beach and Isle of Palms were not far so we got plenty of sunbathing. And there was always Henry's Restaurant and the Officers' Club at the Navy Yard.

As yet, there were no other service women, so we went out with lots of attractive doctors, Marine Corps officers,

Navy officers from the destroyers, even a few dashing British Naval officers. Stewie and a Marine Captain became a couple; but Nell and I lightheartedly dated each other's friends just as we did back in Durham.

Our nursing duties were mostly supervisory because the corpsmen we oversaw were already trained in Navy Medical Corps School. The first time the doctor wrote on the order sheet "Head Privileges", I puzzled for a bit and then went about the ward elevating the bed-heads of my patients. When the senior corpsman asked what I was doing, I told him about doctor's orders. That became the biggest joke in the hospital because in Navy lingo "the Head" is a toilet.

In 1941, only one nurse had weekend duty and she could leave at two-thirty in the afternoon after reporting to the M.O.D. (Medical Officer of the Day). December 7, 1941, I was that weekend nurse on duty in Charleston. Shortly after one p.m., a pharmacist mate from the M.O.D. office came running to my station and said, "The Japanese are bombing Pearl Harbor!" I had heard Orson Welles notorious 1938 *War Of the Worlds* radio broadcast years earlier, so I walked into the office to question his statement. Sure enough, the radio announcer was excitedly describing the Japanese planes and bombs and the sinking of our fleet.

We were all so confused and fearful.

I completed my day's work and I met a friend as previously agreed. We stopped at the Officers' Club, ordered martinis, toasted to the quick defeat of the enemy, then tossed our empty glasses over the deck railing and into the harbor waters.

Monday, December 8, 1941, everyone was at work or at least on duty promptly. Already there seemed to be a more alert determination in the air. Miss Dean asked us to come to her office at noon for President Roosevelt's address to Congress and the nation.

The President, like British Prime Minister Winston Churchill, possessed a magnificent speaking voice. It was an awe-inspiring moment. Roosevelt delivered his "Day of Infamy" speech in which he asked Congress to declare that a State of War now exists between the United States of America and Japan and Germany.

Members of the Armed Forces were required to be in uniform at all times. We nurses had no street uniforms. Miss Dean wired our measurements to Washington. It was not long before we dressed in our Navy Blues. Extra security guards and barriers soon appeared and certain areas of the Navy Yard were marked off-limits. We had to present our identification passes each time we entered or left the gate.

The pace of Charleston quickened and it became crowded overnight. The Ravenels rented their empty second floor bedroom to a young ensign: A Ninety Day Wonder from Harvard.

No more lazy peacetime duty at the hospital. Our hours got longer. As personnel increased, so did our workload and patients. Construction workers filled the area and buildings began going-up in the empty spaces of the Navy Yard. A larger hospital and a nurse residence were also being built.

One evening around seven o'clock, I went into our lounge at the hospital. When I reached inside a closet for another pair of shoes, a hand suddenly grabbed at my wrist. I screamed and ran upstairs to the M.O.D.'s office. At the top of the stairs, several men came toward me and asked what happened. A search was made, but I was told no one was found. A seaman escorted me on all my evening rounds for the next three months.

I must tell you now, that I usually felt quite secure and well protected during my Navy years.

Nell told me the chief of psychiatry told her that a corpsman admitted being the one who frightened me. He received a medical discharge.

When ships were launched at the Charleston Navy Yard, Miss Dean would take a group of nurses to the ceremonies. There were always patriotic songs, the Pledge of Allegiance, speeches by dignitaries, the breaking of champagne bottles over the bows, and the graceful slide of ships into the sea.

Patients began arriving from Pearl Harbor and we learned more about that terrible Sunday morning, but not too much. The sailors seemed hesitant talking about it. A warrant officer told me they were instructed to be discreet. "If the American people knew how disastrous Pearl Harbor was they might lose heart," he said.

In the early fall of 1942, Nell, Stewie, and I received our orders to the Navy Department in Washington. We had shipped our civilian clothing home so packing was no problem. The problem in our nation's capital was housing. At first we lived in one large room at the Roger Smith Hotel within walking distance of Constitution Avenue.

The dispensary was a fairly large facility on the first floor of the Navy Department at 16th Street and Constitution Avenue. Different clinics operated at full speed during the daylight hours and were open for evening emergencies. There were many doctors and corpsmen but only eight nurses.

In the main reception area were an old-fashioned telephone switchboard, two desks, and a few chairs. Two nurses manned this area answering calls for information, requests for home visits and ambulances, and making appointments for the clinics. Our patients were a combination of Navy personnel and dependents, congressmen, and diplomats. Most of my work was at the switchboard or in the women's clinic. I did work an occasional evening shift.

After a week at the Roger Smith, we needed cheaper quarters. With nothing else available, we moved to a boarding house where we received two meals a day. We were still three to a room and shared a small bath with the other tenants on our floor.

Apartment hunting became a must and a real hassle.

Eventually, we learned of a possibility in North West Washington. It was a one-bedroom with a sofa bed in the living room, a small dining room, kitchen, and bath. But first, we had to buy the furniture of the present occupants, and second, we needed a reference from a respectable resident of Washington. Nell's friend from our Charleston days knew Congressman Mendel Rivers of South Carolina personally. That friend met Nell and me on the Capitol steps and escorted us into the South Carolina representative's office. A short while later, we left with his written recommendation and dashed off to 1432 Grand Street North West.

We had our home in wartime Washington.

4.   TROPICAL MOONLIGHT

During World War II, correspondence became extremely important. Servicemen and servicewomen loved receiving mail and in some areas there was little else to look forward to. I wrote to every man who wrote to me. I penned letters to a Marine Lieutenant on Guadalcanal in the South Pacific, a Navy Lieutenant who commanded a task force of minesweepers somewhere in the Pacific, two JG.'s on different destroyers also in the Pacific, and my youngest brother Paul, who was an Army Lieutenant stationed in England at that time.

Scores of people passed through Washington. A former patient of mine called and invited me to dine with him at the Shoreham Hotel's Blue Room, a premier nightspot with delicious food and an orchestra and dance floor. Interspersed with the long gowns and fancy dresses, were numerous men in military uniforms – some of those uniforms were from foreign countries – and there were a fair number of women in uniform. In addition to Army and Navy Nurses, there were now WACS, WAVES, and Women Marines. The city was overcrowded with civilian women and women in uniform.

Nonetheless, it was not devoid of men.

It was fashionable to meet one's date in the lobby of the Willard Hotel, which was convenient to the Navy Department.

We three friends bought custom-made uniforms from a good Washington tailor and made arrangements to sit for portraits by Bachrach, Photographer to Presidents. I mailed one of my large prints home to my parents.

When I reached Union Station a few days before Christmas, the lines were so long, I felt absolutely helpless. Suddenly from somewhere ahead of me, a voice called out, "Sailors, make way for the Lady Ensign!" The smiling man motioned me forward. There were no seats available on the North Carolina bound train; yet again the men arranged a seat for me. This attention was certainly flattering to a simple farmer's daughter.

There was so much gold braid on uniforms in Washington that I constantly saluted as I moved about the streets. One day, I met a man with a sleeve full of dazzling gold braid. Staring at his decorations I snapped-off my best salute unable to determine his rank. He looked at me perplexed at first and then he smiled broadly and saluted me back. Few moments later it dawned on me that he was a Chief Petty Officer with many gold hash marks for long years of good behavior.

He did deserve my salute after all.

The E.E.N.T. (Eye Ear Nose and Throat) clinic at the dispensary was a busy place that winter. Washington winters are so miserably cold and damp. One afternoon, Commander John Ford, the Hollywood movie director, came in with a retinue of officers dressed in Navy aviation greens. His men needed treatment for sinus problems.

One of them, a Clark Gable look-alike, began a conversation with me. Bill told me he was a Hollywood aviation photographer and a member of Commander Ford's group from the USS Hornet aircraft carrier, from which, General Doolittle's planes carried out America's first aerial bomb attack on the Japanese mainland. President Roosevelt announced Doolittle's operation base as "Shangri La" to the American people.

"Like to have dinner with me?" asked Bill. "Take you to the Occidental?"

"Yes. I'd like that," I replied. "Meet you in the Willard Hotel lobby? Say around six?"

"I'll be there waiting."

He has such a beautiful speaking voice and gracious manner...

Bill said he had been detached for duty at Annacostia Naval Station to some kind of secret photographic laboratory. I think he was editing film he took in the South Pacific.

Such an interesting man...

Annacostia was the Naval air station for D.C. and Bill was still there many months later. He knew lots of people and loved introducing me to them. Dan Topping,

24

a Marine officer, and at that time, husband of ice skater Sonja Heine, was with our group at the Statler one night. And it was just good conversation with friends. But the big highlight for me was meeting Lieutenant (jg.) Henry Fonda on a yacht tied up on the Potomac River. Of course, there was the barest of handshakes with Mr. Fonda and then he was out the door.

Bill was a true gentleman and we enjoyed some happy evenings together. Betty, my brother Paul's wife, spent a few days with me, and he was our gallant escort taking us to dinners and to a concert downtown.

One of Bill's friends was a movie soundman also on temporary duty at Annacostia. His wife invited us to Sunday supper, and later I had them to my apartment for dinner using most of that month's meat ration for the ham I baked. During the war many things were rationed – sugar, butter, meat, coffee, shoes, rubber, gasoline. Bill and his friends did not appear to be Hollywood types. They were real people I found nicer than others I'd met.

Although I loved his attention and our happy times together, Bill did not become my big romance.

The summer of 1943, I was promoted to Lieutenant (jg.) and received orders to the Naval Operating Base Roosevelt Roads, Puerto Rico, as chief nurse at the dispensary. Nell had married her Navy Ensign some months earlier and was living back in Charleston. Stewie was left with our apartment at 1432 Grand Street North West.

Before I left Washington for Puerto Rico, the Superintendent of the U.S. Navy Nurse Corps, Captain Sue S. Dauser, asked me to stop by her office. I had never met her before and she was not the expected crisp executive, but a gracious woman who asked me to write her personally once a month with any pertinent news. Leaving the office, her assistant, a Commander, said to me, "You're very young to be in charge of other nurses at a station outside the States. Be careful you don't let that tropical moonlight overwhelm you."

"Of course not," I said.

I took a leave at home before proceeding to Puerto

Rico and got my affairs organized. Earl took me to the local bank where I made arrangements for my monthly allotments to be received into my savings account and my monthly bond, into a safe deposit box. Then I traveled to Charleston and visited my friend Nell and her Navy Lieutenant husband. She was pregnant and Jack was apprehensive about the possibility of sea duty, but they were delighted with thoughts of their baby.

When my train stopped in Miami, I remembered I had neglected to make hotel reservations, and my plane tickets to Puerto Rico necessitated an overnight stay. I took a taxi to the only hotel I'd heard of but no rooms were available. Taking the advice of my cab driver, I ended up in a smaller hotel not far from the airport. It was a rather shabby place but I decided I must find lodging somewhere. I parked a dresser against the locked door and made the best of it.

Before leaving Washington, I was informed that nurses going overseas should take a year's supply of sanitary napkins. I went to Garfinckle's and ordered a large carton of Kotex, about what the saleswoman and I figured adequate. The box had been shipped to Miami. Now I needed to ship it to Puerto Rico.

There was a huge package awaiting me at the railway express office early the next morning. When the porters lifted it they found it so light they could not imagine its contents. "Lady, the size of this box alone will cost you a fortune to ship," they explained to me. "What do you have in here – feathers?"

I told one very cordial man what was inside it.

"Well then, let's open it up and do a bit of re-packing."

We opened the carton, emptied the little boxes, and packed only individual pads, wrapping them tight as possible for shipment.

This time the cost seemed reasonable.

I believed I was becoming a knowledgeable woman and then I learned how wrong I was. Leaving San Juan by car and heading to the Navy base, I saw Kotex boxes in every pharmacy window. I should have known that this was a cosmopolitan city.

How dumb can one person be?

Roosevelt Roads was under construction. It was an immense fenced-in area about fifty miles from San Juan at the far end of the island. A few Navy people were stationed at the base; and hundreds of civilian workmen lived there – but no women. Buildings were being erected and there was all manner of heavy equipment for paving roads and digging ditches. The world's largest breakwater had been started at the tip of land here and crossed the Atlantic toward Vieques, an island almost ten miles away. The breakwater was to accommodate the British Fleet should that country be conquered by Germany. Now it had been abandoned; but Roosevelt Roads continued its buildup of extra large airfields and docks for the American Fleet.

There were four of us nurses occupying a two-bedroom house on Officer's Hill. The base commander lived in one house and the six other houses were each occupied by three to four male officers.

The dispensary was some distance away – a low, wood building with two wards and five private rooms for patients. There was also a large kitchen with a walk-in refrigerator. The personnel included a couple of doctors, a chief pharmacist mate, dozen or more corpsmen, and a grizzled old cook. I soon decided our cook was not that old, but that he was just a rummy.

One morning, there was an explosion in the kitchen.

When the oven was turned on and got hot, a big jug of rum burst apart spraying shards of glass and liquor. Now we knew where the cook hid his bottles for which we'd so often searched. It was way past time for closer supervision. I detailed an Irish-American Nurse, who had recently worked at Cook County Hospital in Chicago, to oversee the kitchen. She had prior experience with alcoholics and did a magnificent job.

Most of our patients did not require intensive care. The sicker ones were sent to the Navy Hospital in San Juan. My office became a gathering spot for the staff. Everyone used it for coffee breaks, and consequently, I, who had never been a coffee drinker, now shared that age-old Navy custom.

The C.O. threw a cocktail party for all officers shortly after my arrival at Roosevelt Roads. Each officer appeared in his or her best dress whites for the command performance – an invitation from the Commanding Officer is a command. After the party, some of us paired-off to continue the evening festivities. Our group went to a Marine Major's house for more drinks and a dinner of sorts. Tom was an attractive, blue-eyed Ensign. He asked me for a date the following evening.

Our friendship soon developed into something deeper. Tom would drop by the house and we'd play cribbage. And I do believe we saw every movie that played at the base amphitheater. We also drove to the nearby hamlets for Spanish movies with English subtitles.

Tom was a supply officer and always had transportation. Occasionally, I would go along when he had business in San Juan. I liked to wander the cobblestone streets, past the shops and into the Old Cathedral. At noon, businesses closed for a two-hour siesta except for the restaurants. Tom and I would meet for lunch at La Mallorquina, the best place in that area. Sometimes we'd drive to the Old Fort El Morro or to Coronado Beach.

Before Christmas, I had really fallen in love with a man for the first time in my life. I was twenty-eight and had dated a fair number of men, but never before had I become so deeply involved. This was different. I was two-feet off the ground. My whole world filled with beauty and wonder. Never gave a thought to heed that older nurse warning me about "tropical moonlight."

Tom asked me to marry him. I said yes. And of course I wrote to my family and friends to share my happiness. He was from an old Massachusetts family with an ancestor who had signed the Declaration of Independence. Tom had graduated from prep school and Yale. Before joining the Navy, he had been in business in Bogotá, Columbia. He was fluent in Spanish and loved that life.

Tom was very special to me.

An Army Colonel invited us to accompany him on his boat when he made inspection of military facilities in Saint Thomas. I spent a gorgeous day on the deck as they trolled for fish without success. We stayed at Blue Beard's Castle, a majestic hilltop retreat with a magnificent view of the town and its charming shops filled with duty-free imports. Tom bought the first items for our future home – a woven white tablecloth and six white napkins. It was handmade in Guatemala and exquisite with lots of rich embroidery.

On our return trip, the Colonel reeled in a rather large barracuda. Tom and I ate at his table in the officer's mess the following night. The entrée was that big fish. It was delicious.

When we got ashore, things were not as nice.

We nurses were unable to rid our house of the hordes of large and troublesome cockroaches. Our maid tried different powders, but the pesky things only seemed to multiply. We kept smaller clothing items in big glass bottles, however, a practically new negligee of mine had been half-eaten by those critters.

Tom brought over a pyrethrum bomb.

We closed the windows and doors, set the device in the center of the dining room, pulled the plug on it, and then quickly locked the doors and went to the base movie. We swept up a gallon can full of dead roaches when we returned several hours later.

After six months at Roosevelt Roads, two nurses received their orders back to the States. Six weeks later, Ellie got her orders to Trinidad. I was the only nurse and the only woman on that huge piece of land. I continued my supervisory duties at the dispensary and spent my evenings with Tom. At first, I didn't mind being alone in the house at night. Later, I became frightened of the tropical noises and I worried about being so isolated. Several times I telephoned Tom in the middle of the night. His bunkmates were annoyed. I don't think he appreciated my late night calls either.

Perhaps I became a bit neurotic with only imaginary fears.

Comedian Bob Hope and his troupe, including Jerry Colonna and Frances Langford, came down to our base to entertain us. Mr. Hope had an infected eye to which I applied compresses for an hour or more. Later during his stage show, he made a few remarks about "Lieutenant Thompson" – his jokes were somewhat suggestive, yet within the bounds of good taste.

Three weeks after Ellie's departure, the newly assigned admiral of our area (Tenth Naval District, I believe) came on inspection tour. I made rounds with him at the dispensary.

"Lieutenant, how many other nurses are stationed at the base beside you?" the Admiral asked me.

"I am the only one, Sir," I answered.

He was aghast. Then turning to his aide he said, "Call my office right now and have orders cut for this young lady to be transferred to San Juan tomorrow!"

That night I packed. I was on my way before noon the next day.

I lived and worked in San Juan for two weeks. Tom and I spoke several times on the telephone, but he came to see me only once. When my new orders arrived, they were for immediate detachment to the hospital in Jacksonville, Florida.

I wrote to Tom from Jacksonville and received a letter from him. And though it was quite a procedure during wartime, I placed a telephone call to him in Puerto Rico. But when three more months passed and I heard nothing from him, I wrote a letter to his mother in Massachusetts (we had never met). I inquired if Tom was all right or if she had heard from him. In return, I received a warm and lovely note telling me she had just received a letter from Tom after his arrival in South America. She said that although he had written about me in earlier letters, he had not mentioned me in the letter she now possessed. Then she graciously asked if she could help in any way. Of course I answered her forthwith, thanking her for the information and her interest in me. "You must do as you wish, however, I would prefer that you not tell Tom I have written you concerning him," I wrote.

My romance and marital plans ended, crushing my self-esteem. But I went on with my life and I learned how to survive.

5. THE ROYAL COACH OF CHILDHOOD DREAMS

Jacksonville was but a brief interlude. I wasn't there long enough to become part of the hospital life. My new orders were to report to the naval air station in Melbourne, Florida as chief nurse at the dispensary.

Melbourne was the air base where Navy fighter pilots trained. Since pilots were commissioned officers, there were a high portion of officers to enlisted men. Many buildings were on base, but I knew only those linked to my living and work – the BOQ and the dispensary, the separate barracks for WAVES and for the enlisted men, and also a large fenced section surrounding the barracks for the German POWs assigned to work-details in that area of Florida. WAVE officers and nurses shared corner suites in the BOQ. On the first floor was a lounge, officers' mess, bar, and cocktail lounge.

The pilots were a mix of Annapolis alumni and reserve officers – former college students with R.O.T.C. credits and three-month graduates of training courses to increase the officer corps: The Ninety Day Wonders.

All of them had completed flight school at Pensacola. They were to be taught combat tactics and the proper takeoff and landing techniques used on aircraft carriers. Later on, each pilot would have temporary duty aboard actual aircraft carriers, practicing and becoming proficient in daylight and nighttime takeoff and landing maneuvers – or else they washed-out and were sent packing for more mundane assignments.

The pilots were intelligent, handsome, physically imposing young men: America's best and brightest. Most of them were happy-go-lucky fellows, with a few more serious combat veterans in their ranks. When they were in training, they were subjected to bed-checks just like prep school boys. Some had money and cars, but others lived modestly.

The dispensary had several wards, one wing of private rooms, operating suite, dental and x-ray departments, and other ancillary areas. There were also clinics that treated Navy wives and children. One time at the daily sick call, a blonde and blue-eyed German POW marched his men into the clinic in strict military formation. He may have been an officer, I suspect.

In November 1944, my youngest brother Paul and his wife Betty came to visit me on their way to Miami. Paul had gone to England in 1942, participated in the North African landings in 1943, and fought at Anzio Beach in Italy. He was part of General Mark Clark's Fifth Army and was promoted to Captain in the Quartermaster Corps. He was offered a major's rank if he would stay in Italy, but he had enough of war. Paul looked great to me, but he was noticeably quieter and more nervous than the boy I last saw in March of 1942.

Paul and Betty had a two-week vacation at the Miami Beach Hotel, courtesy of the Army. When they again stopped by Melbourne on their way home to Cincinnati, both had warm glows on their faces and were relaxed.

My brother Jay called in early January of 1945 to tell me Dad was in the hospital with a heart attack. I obtained emergency leave, departing for North Carolina at once. For a week, I slept on a cot outside his room so I'd be available to assist him in every possible way. We had some good talks about life and our feelings. I was happy to share this time with my father, my strong rock.

Back in Florida, I found a friend.

Fort was an Annapolis graduate from Georgia, with a delightful personality, just filled with the joy of living, and always the center of any group. I never learned how to drive a car. My suite-mate Jeanne did know how to drive. She and I chipped-in and bought an old roadster for one hundred dollars. Fort and I would don our swimsuits, jump into the car, and ride to the nearest beach, usually finding our friends already there. On days off we sometimes spent the entire time cruising the shoreline roads, stopping only for quick dips in the ocean, and then a rest on the hot sands.

Days of laughter when everything was fun.

Some miles away from our base camp was the Castaways, a nightspot where we went dancing. No drinks could be sold after midnight, but if you did order extra alcohol before the witching hour struck, you could go on dancing and drinking for another hour or two or longer. Fort and I were having fun as always one night and decided to stay later. When we left the Castaways a little after three o'clock, he informed me I would have to drive past the Marine checkpoint at the station gate. Before our date, Fort had stuffed his bunk to resemble a sleeping figure to dissuade the bed-checkers.

"Kay, I cannot have my name on that sign-in list," said Fort. "Ya'll surely have to drive us inside."

I agreed. Evidently, some authority figure or such would check the list of names.

We stopped on the roadside and I received my very first driving lesson, brief as it was and in the dead of night. Fort then doubled himself into the car trunk and I got behind the wheel, somehow managing the drive up to the gate. When I showed my identification to the Marine sentry, he gave me a quizzical look. I was extremely nervous and I had trouble with the clutch. There were moments of horrible jerking movements as I pulled through the gate. The guard came toward me to check my actions. I drove away from him, trembling so badly, I could hardly stay in my seat. But I just had to disappear from that Marine's sight.

I let Fort out of the trunk. We laughed in hysterics. "I have never been so frightened in all my born days," he said. "I had visions of being caught by the sentry and then washed-out of fighter school."

"We should be more circumspect, I suppose," I said, holding my sides from laughter.

In the spring of 1945, Fort and his squadron completed their training at Melbourne and received orders to Bakersfield, California. Most pilots took the morning train to Jacksonville, but Fort's good friend, Gene, left his car so we'd have our private goodbye at the beach after I finished work. "Kay, honey, let's ride to Jacksonville. Ya'll can come back by train later tonight."

V-E Day in May of 1945 was an occasion to celebrate, but Navy people were only partially relieved by our victory in Europe. Most Navy personnel, especially the pilots, were stationed in the Pacific during World War II. It was still a dangerous world.

Headquarters sent a second notice asking nurses to apply for flight duty. I ignored the January notice because of Dad's illness. But this time, he was doing well and I really loved everything about the air station – the pilots, the airplanes. It was an elite group and I wanted to serve with them.

There was a high level of excitement at Melbourne when we heard the news that atom bombs had been dropped on Hiroshima and Nagasaki. No one seemed to know anything about these weapons prior to this happening. The reports of the utter devastation of whole cities and thousands of their inhabitants – whom we considered enemies – caused immediate cheering and toasts to the final demise of Hirohito and his bloodthirsty empire. We did celebrate. But we did not gloat. Many people had been killed on both sides of the war. And it is not right to mock the vanquished.

Japan capitulated on August 14, 1945.

We all wondered how our duties and lives would change with the ending of hostilities. I was relieved and especially happy for Fort who was nearing the end of his fighter pilot training in California. He no longer had to face death in aerial combat.

I was promoted to Lieutenant. Jeanne and I had orders to report to flight school at N.A.S. Alameda, California. I spent a week at home with my folks before heading west. Dad had retired from active farming because of his heart condition. My second youngest brother Jay and his wife Ruth and their small daughter Harriet, now had an apartment in our home. Jay assumed responsibility for the farm. A black family moved into a small house that Dad had built on the edge of our woods, and helped my brother work the land. My father's health had seemingly improved, and now my parents had the support they needed with Jay and his family there.

I stopped in Cincinnati to see my brother Paul and his wife Betty and their two-month old baby on my way to California. Paul awaited his release from active duty.

Jeanne and I met in Chicago and flew together to Alameda on September 2, 1945. During the flight our pilot announced the Japanese had just signed the formal surrender on the USS Missouri battleship in Tokyo Bay.

V-J Day at last! The bloodiest war in world history ended.

Alameda Airbase was a beehive of activity with the flight school only a part of the action. Mary Ellen O'Conner, a R.N. and the senior flight attendant at United Air Lines, later dubbed "the most flyingest woman in the world", headed our group. There were also flight surgeons, technicians, and instructors. We spent time training in flight simulators to experience the effects of gravity, turbulence, and oxygen deprivation. We reviewed medical facts that might affect our patients and us during flight, and emphasis was also placed on ditching procedures. Everything was interesting and vitally important to our mission.

On off-duty time, we ferried across the bay to San Francisco and rode cable cars up and down its hilly streets. One time, two chaplains took us to the Top Of The Mark, a revolving cocktail lounge, on the highest floor of the Mark Hopkins Hotel on Nob Hill. It had breathtaking views of the city at dusk. At a mansion a few blocks away, an older woman welcomed us inside her Open House Sundays For Navy Officers.

The Alameda officers' mess was a good place to meet old friends and make new ones. One day, I saw Dr. Ross, the chief of obstetrics at Watts Hospital in Durham. Another time, I met a classmate of Fort's. When the USS Saratoga docked with thousands of men returning from the Pacific, we went to the harbor and cheered them.

Fort's friend Doug invited me to go with him and another couple to the Golden Gloves boxing matches at the Cow Palace in San Francisco. That night, idling outside the door of the BOQ, was the biggest and most luxurious car I had ever seen. Sitting at the wheel of the Duisenberg was a good-looking Lieutenant Commander with his arm around his date, a WAVE Officer. The top was down exposing a dashboard that resembled the cockpit of an R5D. I felt a mile away from the couple in the front seat; a fairy-tale princess riding in the royal coach of childhood dreams. Driving over the Bay Bridge through San Francisco streets, people gaped at us. I felt special. But it was an artificial evening. And I did not enjoy the bloody fisticuffs at the Cow Palace.

A large group of us celebrated graduation and the receiving of our "Wings" at a San Francisco nightspot. One of the flight surgeons told the maître d' we were headed to the South Pacific. The emcee announced our presence and our destination to the crowd. We stood at his urging to thunderous and sustained applause.

That last weekend, we nurses hitched plane rides to Los Angeles, where we had reserved rooms at the Ambassador Hotel. Fort and I had been writing every few weeks. I called him in Bakersfield and he said if I found a date for his friend Gene they would drive down and take us to dinner the next night.

The men looked spectacular in their dress whites. They had reserved a table at Ciro's in Hollywood where we were treated like royalty. Fort and I were really dancing around the floor and bumped into Carmen Miranda and Xavier Cugat. I was so preoccupied with the evening's gaiety I never even noticed them until our collision. The famous Latin duo sort of smiled through their grimaces. I was embarrassed and Fort thought it hilarious. Just like old times together, yet now, a more deluxe setting for our frivolity.

Back at the Ambassador, we wandered the grounds for a while, not wanting to part. But the men had a long drive back to Bakersfield and were to fly that very morning. We said our goodbyes and I promised I'd call Fort whenever my evacuation flights landed. Meanwhile, we would continue to write.

On October 10, 1945, the newest class of flight nurses and corpsmen flew to John Rogers Airfield in Honolulu. I gazed out the airplane windows at the glories of Diamond Head, the volcanic mountains, and the surfers skimming atop waves toward sandy beaches in bright morning sunshine.

The nurses' residence was a large quonset hut. Its reception area included a desk for the Marine guard who logged us "in" and "out". Our rooms were sparsely furnished, with three to a room at first. Later I roomed alone. We had communal showers and heads. Inside of our fenced-in area was a backyard that we used as our tanning salon. Officers' mess was not far away and there was a snack bar even closer. The nurses already living there were quite courteous and helpful in giving us the lowdown about Hawaiian duty.

We took the bus to Honolulu and on to Waikiki Beach in the afternoons. In the evenings, we were invited to dances at Ford Island and at the Marine base adjoining our compound. Bob Crosby's Band, all strapping young Marines, provided the music when I first lived in Hawaii. The officers drove us around Punch Bowl and up to Mount Tantalus on starry nights, and then back home in the wee hours. On occasion, we managed several dates during the day and evening – lunch with Navy pilots; afternoon swims with Marines; and perhaps dinner with the Army, if we had no previous reservations.

A large mansion at Kahana Bay had been set aside for Navy women's recreational use. Groups of us would stay there for a few days at a time. We took the bus to the mansion; crossing the Pali, a magnificent mountain pass on the far side of Oahu. A staff of servants were left on the mansion grounds. We paid all of one dollar and fifty cents per-day to cover our expenses. The backyard was a sandy beach with the best bodysurfing on the island. I went to the Kahana Bay Mansion often before its owners returned from the mainland.

November 16, 1945, I made my first air evacuation flight as a working crewmember. Twenty patients were already in litters rigged against the bulkheads as I climbed aboard. The other crewmembers were the pilot, co-pilot, navigator, flight attendant, and a corpsman.

My equipment consisted of a small trunk containing IVs, plasma, surgical instruments, dressings, medical supplies, and a select supply of medications. I carried a sleeping bag and leather flight jacket into which I placed my pocketsize cribbage board. I wore the aviation green slack suit with a visor cap; my wings and rank insignia with the ribbons were also part of my uniform.

My first flight to Alameda was uneventful. However, at times we flew almost to E.T.P. (Estimated Turning Point), then returned to base; for sudden storms or strong headwinds engendered fuel depletion, making it a risky deal to go onward.

Today was pleasant.

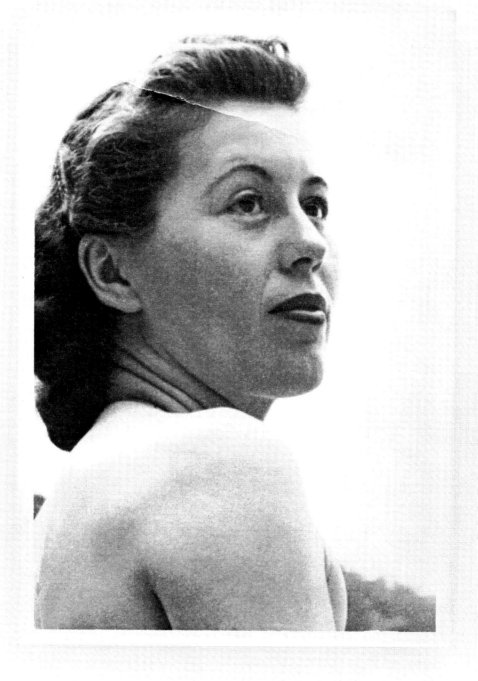

6. TORPEDO JUICE

Next morning in Alameda, I telephoned home and spoke with Mother and Dad. Then I attempted to call Fort in Bakersfield, but could not reach him.

The following afternoon I telephoned for him again. The woman who answered my call at his squadron's office seemed agitated, stammered a bit, and then asked if I would like to speak to Fort's commanding officer.

It was so strange to me that I in turn became nervous.

The Commanding Officer asked my name and the nature of my relationship with Fort. Never had anyone questioned me like this.

"Fort and I are old friends from Melbourne," I said. "I'm a flight nurse in from Honolulu."

"Lieutenant Thompson, Fort has gone down in the drink," he said in a somber voice. "We have aircraft searching for him at this very moment. But I must tell you, we don't have much hope here."

I heard radios crackling in the background, sounds of the desperate voices of many pilots trying to find him. I was speechless for a moment and shaken. And then, "No, no, no, not Fort! Not him! Lord, not him!" I cried out.

Why did this happen to such a vital and loving young man? The war is supposed to be over...

A week later, I received a thick letter in Fort's handwriting. My heart broke. The date posted was the same day I had landed at Alameda. It was filled with his thoughts, what he'd been doing, and his remembrances of our fun times together.

His death was real, and it was sad. But I am thankful and happy because I knew and loved him.

Three weeks later, on the evening of December 20, 1945, I had a call from base communications saying a radiogram had been sent to me and they would send a driver to bring me to the administration building.

The driver led me to a chair in the office and a chief petty officer handed me the wire. My father had died. It was too much. I broke down and wept. The men were solicitous, offering to make travel arrangements for the trip back home to Carolina.

I could get to the West Coast with little problem; however, I doubted my resilience in taking such a long and torturous journey home without a companion. With the war ended and Christmas fast approaching, the hordes of service people still returning from the Pacific, were determined to spend the 1945 holiday season with their loved ones. I wired my family expressing my deepest love, my grief, and my inability to be with them.

Friends and fellow nurses helped me with my sorrow. They were caring, seeing to it that I always had a companion during those holidays. They sent flowers to Dad's funeral and I personally wired his favorite – a dozen red rosebuds. I wrote long letters to Mother and each of my brothers and to my sister.

It was the saddest and loneliest Christmas I ever spent. Dad's love was an Absolute. Upon his love, I had always depended. His death was the major loss of my life.

The scheduling nurse decided I needed to keep busy. I was constantly flying for the next two months. Usually, we flew one trip to the States and the next flight to Guam or another Pacific island.

En route to Guam, we would refuel at Johnston Island, a tiny dot amidst the big ocean. Once, when we had an overnight stay there because of engine trouble, I stayed inside a tiny quonset and had a Marine sentry patrolling around it all night long.

Kwajalein was a narrow strip of sand and rock just three miles long. Prior to its liberation from the Japanese, it had been a beautiful wooded island. Navy ships had so heavily shelled it that now only one scrawny tree remained.

The Kwajalein living quarters were the poorest I ever occupied in my life. A Red Cross woman was bitten on the face by a rat. I slept with the lights on. I wasn't sure it would help, but I figured the glare might frighten the varmints or at least I'd be able to see them coming. Showers were available only at specified hours; the water was a rusty brown color and just a trickle at that. The food was either canned or dehydrated and the butter rancid.

I did like the fresh baked bread when it was toasted, but I had to pluck dead insects from it before eating. Two Marines with holstered guns sat at the reception desk. Nurses were allowed to leave the area only with two chaperones, one to carry the M1 rifle. We had to sign "in" and "out" and our escorts signed their names in affirmation. Recreation meant a nearby beach during the days, and the officers' club in the evenings.

When I was at Kwajalein, we received reports that a tidal wave hit the Big Island of Hawaii. Since Kwajalein was only three-feet above sea level, our ships anchored offshore. All the women except for me, were taken by dinghy to board a vessel. Our operations officer sent a jeep to the women's quarters to bring me to the hangar. I awaited the evacuation plane with tropical winds raging outside.

But disaster missed us after all.

Now, Guam is a much larger island and populated with natives and U.S. military personnel. The same numbers of flight nurses were stationed here as in Honolulu. Sometimes, I remained in Guam for a week or more. One time I ran into a friend of mine from Puerto Rico, a Marine Major named Don.

In 1946, I flew with a seventeen-year-old, clean-cut sailor from Kwajalein to Oahu. He was totally blind, having consumed a small amount of torpedo juice with a few of his shipmates who had assured the boy they'd made it safe to drink. They were all dead now, save for this unhappy teenager, alive, though blinded forever. I felt for him – so sad, so young, a sweet innocent.

My friend Rennie and I hitched a plane ride to Hilo for a couple of days. We stayed at a hotel there and visited the Volcano House, walking right up to the edge of the fiery pit. The next day we took a taxi to Akaka Falls.

I landed at Midway Island to pickup patients. Its runways were overrun with goony birds. These were the large albatross I'd read about in *The Ancient Mariner*. The birds were a hazard to our planes, sometimes causing accidents. Ground crews buzzed their jeeps up and down the runways just before takeoffs, attempting to scatter them. The goony birds would waddle down the runways and take flight the same way airplanes do, so they were loathe to leave its flat surface. I walked by them and watched some doing mating dances while others sat comfortably in nests. A crewmember gave me a photograph he'd taken of them. I also purchased a clever book with goony bird illustrations titled: *Midway Verse Or Worse*. I enjoy reading it from time to time.

March of 1946, I was promoted to Lieutenant Commander and presented decoration ribbons including: American Defense (that was for my pre-Pearl Harbor Service), American and Asiatic-Pacific Theater, and a Presidential Unit Citation for our air evacuation squadron.

We were again permitted to wear our civilian clothes when off-duty. I joined the Navy in May of 1941 and I had not spent my money on any fashionable attire.

I really shopped after landing in San Francisco.

At I. Magnin's department store, I bought a mink scarf with three plump Baum Marten skins, a couple of smart suits, two three-quarter length coats, oodles of accessories, and two exquisite long gowns for any formal occasions. And I purchased a few pieces of jewelry – an unusually carved jade ring and ivory earrings and pin at Ming's in Honolulu upon my return from the mainland.

My social life was terrific – no one special person, but always someone there to meet my plane.

I took an interesting flight to Samoa via Canton Island, an exotic tropical green and mountainous paradise. The thatch-roof dwellings reminded me of Somerset Maugham's *Rain*. There were modern buildings too. The male waiters at our Samoan quarters wore a sort of sarong.

Hmm. Now that garment does have a special name... But I have forgotten it.

By 1947, Honolulu had returned to its prewar status. It was not the same. None of the places where thousands of Americans had covered the globe, would ever be the same again. Nor would we. The Royal Hawaiian Hotel was no longer a facility for submarine officers. It was refurbished and again catered to wealthy tourists. Hotels and clubs were built and we had new and elegant spots for dining and dancing. Navy families came back to Honolulu and many reserve officers returned to their civilian lives on the mainland. Many of the nurses went back home too.

When I got my stateside orders in July 1948, I felt a bit sad. This paradise had been my Navy home longer than any other place.

7. THE VENDOR'S PRICE

My friend Lou and I were transferred to the exact same location. We flew to Washington, D.C., where my brother Jay and his family met us. Lou flew on to her North Carolina home and I visited with Jay for a few days. Mother was with Paul in Cincinnati, so I flew up there.

I had been away from my family for two years. It was a real occasion for the Thompsons. Mother and I went back to Carolina after a few days in Cincinnati. My brothers Earl and Jay and their families awaited our arrival at the farm. My sister Mary Wood and her husband Deke and their three children drove over from Chapel Hill.

Mother was a southerner from the old school.

"Catherine, why in heaven's name are you so dark?" she asked me. "I do declare you might be asked to sit in the back of the bus." I laughed because complete strangers in San Francisco had stopped me on the streets to compliment me on my gorgeous tan. I'd been in tropical areas for more than three years and was proud of that tan. And I thought my skin tone quite natural with that reddish-gold hue no matter what anyone said.

N.A.S. Patuxent River, Maryland, was a huge base sixty miles south of Washington. It was a testing site for naval aviation. VR-1, our squadron, was the wing for East Coast Navy Air Transport including mail, cargo, priority passengers, and evacuation. Flight nurses were stationed at Patuxent and there were many pilots. I knew a lot of them having shared hours in flight and a bit of beach time. There were apartments on the base for families, a BOQ for single male officers, and a women's quarters for Navy Nurses and WAVE Officers.

My flights took me up and down the East Coast corridor and sometimes into the Midwest or Southwest. I also had regular stops at Guantanamo Bay, Cuba. There were trips to Port Lyautey in French Morocco by way of Newfoundland and the Azores. I did tire on the long flights. But I never tired of the excitement of meeting new people and visiting different places.

In early January 1948, I landed in Port Lyautey, Morocco. I was assigned a first floor bedroom at the BOQ with no bathroom and no door locks. I questioned this, and was directed to the men's head and showers on the second floor. Evidently, they were unprepared for women. Lyautey was a French base and those young French soldiers smiled at my dismay.

At dinner that evening, our pilots invited me to accompany them to Rabat the next morning. The countryside looked like my old Bible pictures. Our guide was a streetwise Arab teenager, who spoke good English. We walked through the Medina section of the city with its exotic smells, sights, languages, and activities.

In the French area were several fancy boutiques.

When I told our Arab guide that I needed to exchange some of my American dollars, he offered to go and do it for me. I handed him forty dollars. The pilots gasped and swore I'd never see my money or our guide again. We waited and waited until I almost believed them, but then, he returned with a fist full of francs. I bought French perfume and a beautiful porcelain doll. Collecting dolls had become my hobby since my Puerto Rico days.

On our return trip to the base we stopped for drinks. An Arab vendor approached our table. The pilots suggested I bargain with him for an item in his tray. I picked up an odd turquoise bracelet. "How much?" I asked him.

"Twelve hundred francs," he said.

I turned away.

"How much will you pay?" he asked me.

"Six hundred," I said foolishly.

"Sold," the vendor said, a sly grin stretching across his face.

I sat there bewildered. I never expected to buy that ugly thing. The pilots howled at my predicament. My dilemma was the highlight of their day. I had to pay the vendor's price. And to this very hour I have an ugly and expensive bracelet as a memento of my quick tongue and careless decision-making process.

Back at the base, I found I'd been moved into a room in the captain's family apartment. Everyone in our group was in great spirits and we relaxed over dinner and a few more drinks. Several hours later, I realized the others had left me and another pilot alone. This most attractive man walked me to my room and then we paused at the door. He bent over slightly to me and I reached upward for a simple goodnight embrace. But his kiss was electric, achingly sweet. And I dreamed erotic dreams all night, awaking certain neither of us could possibly forget last night's overwhelming sensations.

A short while later, I got new orders for an extended flight to Trinidad, Guantanamo Bay, and the Panama Canal Zone.

Secretary Stuart Symington, of the newly created U.S. Air Force, was making an inspection tour of both Army and Navy bases in the Caribbean. VIPs would meet him at the air stations, and as senior flight nurse, I was to accompany our NATS captain on his travels. The captain's wife suggested that I pack one long dress for a formal dinner in Trinidad.

I stayed at the nurses' quarters in Trinidad, but I spent the daylight hours on the beach with my crew. I was chauffeured that evening to the formal dinner and seated between Secretary Symington's aide and his pilot and directly across from the Navy Captain from Pautexant. I felt special to be in this glittering company, however it was not an especially exciting time. And I wondered when I had begun to feel my life should always be this way.

In Panama, I stayed at the apartment of the NATS operations officer and his wife. Next morning, I needed a shampoo and remained behind while everyone else went to the pool. Walking from the shower into the living room, I saw a young Panamanian man standing by a lamp table, holding several loose dollar bills in his hand. I had absolutely no fear at the moment of discovery and marched a bit closer to him. "What are you doing here?" I asked him. "Where did you get that money?"

"Por favor, no tell anyone," he stammered, handing the money to me.

"Empty your pockets," I commanded him. He did, producing a few more dollars. "Is that all?" I asked him.

The frightened youth removed a single dollar from his cigarette pack, gave it to me, and then backed away toward the door. I followed and I locked it behind him. Then I turned and saw a partially opened silver box atop the dining table, half-filled with more cash. I thought I might not mention the incident because the boy had returned everything. But, I decided to report what happened and telephoned the captain.

Moments later the Captain, Commanding Officer, and Marines filled the room. I was still in my robe and my hair was dripping wet. After I dressed, they escorted me below to identify the frightened intruder, which I did. Although we were to depart the following morning, the authorities had arranged a speedy trial and I was to testify.

The federal judge, an American with jurisdiction in the Canal Zone, presided over court. I told my story in his cramped chambers packed with U.S. military personnel. The Panamanian was given a one-year sentence. I felt sorry for him, but my pilot friends were surprised that he had not stabbed me and advised me never to return there.

I wonder how my actions affected that boy's life. Did I do the right thing?

Tess, another flight nurse, and I hitched a plane ride to Bermuda for five days leave in March. We stayed in Hamilton at the Bermudiana Hotel, shopped on Front Street for English sweaters, and then took horse driven carriages for our sightseeing excursions. One day we journeyed to Saint Georges, the older and more picturesque part of the island. I bought prints from a local artist and brought them back to Pautexant for suitable framing.

Tom, the man of my Moroccan fantasies, telephoned me and asked if I could schedule myself on a specific flight to Port Lyautey. He remembered me. And nothing would prevent me from making the trip.

Tom and I went with a group of other pilots to a nightspot not far from base. There were belly dancers, a few other acts, and music and dancing. I sat entranced, experiencing for real the stories I'd read as a farm child: *Ali Baba and the Forty Thieves*, magic carpet rides, concubines adorned in purple silk veils performing in their Sheikh's harem. It was very romantic. And I floated on air.

On the return flight we had engine trouble. Tom and I stayed overnight at Lagens Air Field in the Azores.

Winding streets in the village were paved in colorful tiles.

It is true! Though stars were surely in my eyes, also was certain truth.

I purchase bottles of Mateus Rosé, a fine Portuguese wine, and sets of Madeira embroidered linen tablecloths and napkins. I love the quaint charm of this place. But most of all I love this particular man. I promise myself I will be cool this time, expecting nothing from him. I will never actually pursue him. I will wait for him to make the moves. I keep these promises to myself. It is often difficult to do.

A week later, I landed at Guantanamo Bay on temporary duty, flying inter-island hops to airlift patients from the field stations to the larger hospitals. On my second day in Cuba, the man in my life called again. Tom took some time-off and flew down to be with me.

He flew along with me on evacuation runs. There were many hours just for us. We went to movies on the base and spent hours on the porch at the nurses' quarters. We walked about the station and took a train ride to a Cuban village some miles away. Another night we attended a grand party given by an officer and his young bride. We were together almost a week. It was a magical time, a vacation for me. He was dear and caring. I hoped I was loved and beautiful in Tom's eyes. I desperately wanted it to be true.

In July, The Constitution, a spanking new two hundred passenger Lockheed built plane, was to be commissioned at National Airport in Washington. My friend Fran and I were scheduled for the ceremonial duty. We stood under its huge wings and posed for the press photographers. Next morning, we flew on The Constitution with Navy and Lockheed VIPs to the formal opening of Idlewild Airport in New York City. We acted as hostesses showing the dignitaries through the big plane.

Each evening a stretch limousine arrived to chauffeur us to the Hotel Lexington in Manhattan, and each morning it picked us up there and returned us to the Idlewild. In our limousine group were four Lockheed engineers and crew chiefs. On our first evening, the engineers invited Fran and I to dinner at a cozy French restaurant on the East Side. The crew chiefs had us to dinner the following night at the Hotel Lexington's Hawaiian Room.

They were all interesting men.

Back at Patuxent, we invited our Lockheed friends to join us and a few other nurses at the Officers' Club. Just as my peach cobbler dessert arrived, I had a call. My lover from Morocco wanted to see me now. I left cash with Fran to help pay the check and then I went to meet Tom. Our dinner had been fun, however, I desired to be near the one who gave me feelings of comfort and safety and happiness.

The pilots had heavier schedules now with flights to Greece and Italy. Weeks went by before Tom and I saw each other again. We continued our quiet evenings inside the screened porch. On a crisp autumn day, we joined another couple for a drive along Skyline Drive in Shenandoah National Park – a rare and lovely day.

The second week of December, I was sent to Corpus Christie, Texas, for two weeks temporary duty. I flew on from there to Pensacola, Mobile, San Antonio, and Houston. Then orders arrived for another two-week stint in Jacksonville.

I received new orders returning me to hospital duty at the Naval Medical Center in Bethesda, Maryland. Sure enough a blow! I had enjoyed such wonderful years at the air stations and as a flight nurse. I disliked the idea of "real" nursing again.

At Patuxent River, a day before I was to checkout, my special friend called. "Kay, do you still want to buy a car?" Tom asked me. "A pilot I know has one for sale. He bought another car in Cuba and had it shipped at Uncle Sam's expense. He doesn't need the one he has stateside."

"May I see it first?"

It was a two-door Studebaker with red upholstery. I loved it. Tom and his pilot friend met me at the bank and I handed over a check and received the necessary documents.

"I'll have to ask my brother Jay to come up and drive me back to North Carolina," I mentioned to Tom.

"Nonsense, Kay, I'll drive you down there," he said.

"And I will pay for your plane ticket back to Washington."

"Deal."

Although I was leaving flight nursing, I did not feel unhappy that sunny April morning in 1949. I was joyous. Tom and I would spend all day together, traveling through the Southland.

"My mother is going to marry again when I get back to the farm," I said.

"Really?"

At that exact moment, I realized Tom and I had never questioned one another or volunteered much information about our respective families. We only had present thoughts and feelings, or at least I did. We had avoided probing into each other's backgrounds.

Tom and I stopped briefly for lunch and gasoline, arriving at Mary Wood and Deke's home in Chapel Hill before sunset. My sister prepared an excellent spaghetti supper. However, there was some controversial discussion about Mother's impending marriage. Mary Wood and Deke were opposed to it. I had never met Mother's prospective groom, and so I could judge him not. In the midst of exchanging our views, my brother-in-law made an uncalled for remark, to which I took instant exception.

"How dare you speak of my mother like that!"

We abruptly left the table. Tom was also offended by Deke. "Kay, I don't know your mother. But I am so damn angry at what that fellow said, I really want to knock him down for you!"

My champion senses my reactions; cares for my feelings. Kinfolk ride with us to the airport. I give my lover his ticket away from me. My world is in disarray. I feel a bit ill. I want to throw my arms around him; yet I must not in front of this audience. Holding hands too briefly, then saying goodbye. See you again in a few days. I stand as a wooden soldier, willing my feet to not run after him. He walks away, turns once, gazes at me. Gone forever.

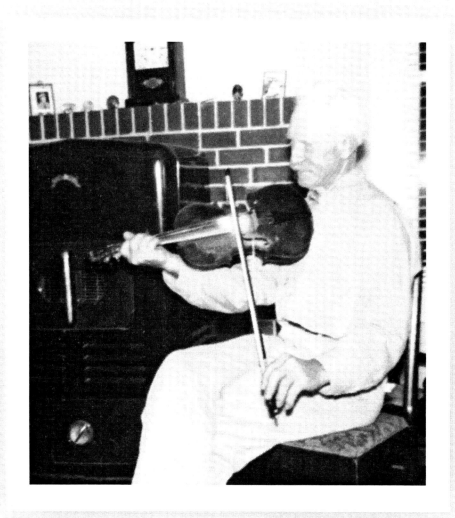

8. DRIVING LESSONS

The next morning Deke drove me to the farm. During the trip, he gave me many pointers about driving, stopping every half-hour to let me sit behind the wheel to try my hand at shifting the gears, deploying the brakes, and using the turn signals. Despite the other night's previous unpleasantness, I was fond of Deke. He had always been generous and gracious to me, and he was a natural born teacher. It was good of him to drive me out to the Piedmont, for Deke surely loathed his return bus trip back to Chapel Hill.

I met my mother's fiancé later that afternoon. "Mister Will" Wetmore was a handsome and well-dressed widower with beautiful snow-white hair. He was eight years older than Mother at seventy and rather shy, but as soon as he sat down for coffee he said, "Well, Catherine, some of your family aren't too happy about me marrying your mother. But I want you to know, that I love her and all I want is to take care of her and make her happy."

I had a tear in my eye and I saw one just like it in his. "Mister Will, that is everything we want," I said. "If you make Mother happy, we'll all love you."

Mother and I shared a few private days together. She had known Mister Will and his family since childhood, and was very sure of herself and of what she planned to do.

That was Mother.

My oldest brother Earl and his wife Sara Frances and their boy William came down, but remained in their rooms during the ceremony. Earl just could not bear to watch her wed another man. Mother and Mister Will exchanged vows in our parlor. A young Presbyterian minister, who once lived in our home for a few months, officiated instead of my brother Earl, who was also a Presbyterian minister.

We waited for Jay to come by bus from Greensboro. Sara Frances and I prepared a cold buffet and set the table for the honeymooners. Mother and Mister Will were back before sunset from their car ride to the nearby mountains.

Jay drove my car and me to Greensboro that afternoon. His wife had arranged driving lessons for me. I spent the next week practicing driving and learning about cars. I got my license! And then Jay drove me back to Washington.

Bethesda is a suburb of Washington and the home of the Navy Medical Center that included the hospital, schools of medicine, dentistry, administration, research projects, and other medical technologies.

I started down to Patuxent with two younger nurses the first Sunday after returning from Carolina. We rode merrily along until we reached Waldorf, Maryland. I was in overdrive, my foot off the accelerator, when traffic came to a sudden stop. I pressed my foot too hard onto what I thought was the brake. But it was the gas pedal I'd pressed and we plowed into the line of cars in front of us.

The car did stop of course, but there was loud clashing of metal and shattered glass. One of my passengers received a small but deep gash on her cheek. The other nurse had a fractured nose and wrist. I had a few small facial contusions and lacerations, some bad bruises that just missed both my kneecaps, and a very sore chest from hitting the steering wheel.

A gracious and efficient state trooper directed traffic around our collision site. People were leaving church services to my right, and there was much confusion. Despite the fact my license and car insurance papers were only temporary ones, that nice policeman merely shook his head. He felt sorry for me because I told him it was my fault and exactly what had happened. He walked us to a doctor's office beside the church and then he returned to deal with the cars damaged by my stupidity. After we received first aid, I telephoned the Bethesda Naval Hospital and asked that a car be sent to pick us up.

Back at Bethesda, we were thoroughly checked and hospitalized overnight. The Washington Post showed a photograph of another accident at that same location a few days later. A man had died there because the steering wheel had crushed his chest.

Oh, my. I am fortunate indeed.

My nursing assignment was to Tower 16 during the day shifts. When I did night duty, I supervised Towers 14 through 17. Tower 17 had only five rooms and they were kept available for our country's most important officials. Admiral Leahy and Admiral King were my patients there. When the powers that be learned I hadn't done any night duty for several years, I was assigned those hours for most of the summer.

Vice President Alben W. Barkley came to visit his good friend, the Senate Majority Leader, Wallace H. White Jr., one night and started up a conversation with me – the true politician that he was. We discovered that his mother or grandmother was a distant cousin of Grandma Fleming from Rowan County. He said goodbye to me. And then he kissed me on my lips. "That one's 'cause we're kissin' cousins," he said, as the elevator doors closed. The young corpsman on duty nearly fainted.

My social life was just this short of nil. I longed for the friendly group I knew back at Patuxent. It took about a month, but I drove my car again. Off-duty, I practiced driving two hours a day. I would drive to Frederick, Maryland, turn around and then drive back. I was too shaky at first to ask anyone to risk his or her lives with me behind the wheel.

Gradually, I regained a bit of confidence.

Gene, Fort's friend from Melbourne and that last star-crossed night in Hollywood, called me one Sunday. He was still the same steady and friendly man, and now a Navy Commander. Somehow he had tracked me down.

We went to Olney, Maryland, to a dinner theater. Although we were happy to meet again, the only thing we had in common was our mutual love of Fort.

"Kay, were you the woman who telephoned for Fort when he went down?" Gene asked me.

"Yes."

"All of us were struck by the coincidence of your call at that exact moment. I was certain the caller had to be you."

Our time together seemed somber in comparison to the gaiety of those golden moments when Fort was the driving force behind all that we did and felt.

This evening was the goodbye we needed sharing to put Fort to rest.

9. THE SIGNIFICANCE OF SOUTHERN KINSHIP CLAIMS

In October 1949, I received orders to be the liaison nurse at the Military Sea Transport Service in New Orleans. I had never heard of it before. This proved to be an Army outfit at the New Orleans Port of Embarkation that the Navy was in the process of absorbing. These were Merchant Marine ships attached to the Army; but ships really are the responsibility of our Navy. Almost anything sounded better to me than hospital night duty at Bethesda. Off I went for my first completely independent duty – the lone Navy Nurse at an Army station.

I stopped by the farm and then Birmingham, Alabama, before traveling on to New Orleans. I felt insecure driving over the twenty-five mile long Lake Pontchartrain Bridge, with its narrow lanes built of wood planks. However, I had no problems finding Canal Street and the Saint Charles Hotel. And I had finally learned to make my reservations in advance.

After checking into my room, I called Anne, a nurse I knew from Bethesda. Her husband Bill, a chief purser for United Fruit Company, happened to be in downtown New Orleans at that very hour, so she asked him to stop by and bring me to their home for dinner. Bill left port within days and Anne invited me to live with her until I found an apartment.

Military Sea Transport officers were in a warehouse on the docks. Its personnel were half Army and half Navy. Our medical officer was a doctor I'd known only slightly from my Charleston days in 1942. He was the younger brother of the husband of a favorite cousin of my mother.

Now, you must understand the significance of southern kinship claims, for we do have dozens and dozens of cousins. In the South, if a person claims kinship to another, it cements relationships, making them much more immediate and special. Anyway, Mother's favorite cousin's husband's younger brother and his wife invited me to share Thanksgiving dinner with them – certainly a gracious thing to do.

I wrote regular reports to McCoy, a friend since Charleston, now a Commander in the office of the Director of Navy Nurses. I loathed submitting reports through channels and by sending information direct to McCoy at the head office, I avoided the pitfalls of dealing with Navy bureaucracy and its never-ending spools of red tape.

An Army transport ship was to sail for Panama filled with military dependents. I was assigned to the crew along with two Army nurses already on the ship's roster. The other personnel were Merchant Marines with the exception of our medical group. There were morning and evening sick calls aboard ship. Most of the women and children patients required seasickness remedies and there were other illnesses to treat.

When we docked in Panama, we were off-duty until new passengers boarded for the return trip to New Orleans. Bill's ship happened to be in port too and he invited me ashore for lunch. Late afternoon, I returned to shower and change before going ashore again that evening with a group from our ship. As I adjusted my dress straps, a hand reached through the porthole and grabbed my shoulder. I screamed and ran toward my cabin door. There was a loud knock as I reached for the doorknob. An officer heard my cry and had rushed to my aid.

There was a flurry of activity to find the offender.

Although my porthole was open, the drapes were drawn. It had never occurred to me someone might push them aside. And it was reasonable to assume the interloper was someone with access to the staterooms and to the deck outside them.

The following morning the Captain, an imposing yet polite man, sent for me to meet him near the ship's bow. He apologized for the incident and told me that the miscreant had been found. "He's your cabin boy," he said.

"The one who brings me ice and baskets of fruit everyday?"

"Yes, the very same one."

Captain then said he had talked the night before with his friend, the same judge who had heard the case of my Panamanian intruder years ago. "Judge remembers you," he said.

"Oh, does he now?"

They thought it best to lock the young man aboard ship for our voyage home and then discipline him back in New Orleans. "Unless you disagree."

"Captain, I believe that solves it just fine," I said.

"Good."

"What will become of him?" I asked.

"Probably only fire him, I'd think."

Perhaps these incidents happened to other nurses but I wonder why I never heard of it. Then again, I did not go around telling these stories either. I don't believe it was my fault anyway. Nevertheless, it is a bit puzzling to me.

Days off, I strolled alone through the French Quarter wandering into gift shops that sold trinkets and candies, passing the girlie shows with their doorway barkers enticing customers to enter, beyond earshot of the ragtime jazz coming from the honky tonks, and into an adjoining area of picturesque residences with lacy wrought iron balconies and shuttered windows. Then I'd take my lunch at a romantic café before returning to my apartment.

On an occasional evening, I dated the assistant manager of my apartment building. He was a native of New Orleans and took me to Louis Primo's, Pat O'Brien's, and one evening to Brennan's. That was the extent of my social life; save for the night I invited Anne and another girl to be my guests at Antoine's, which is truly one of the great restaurants. Even without men, it was a treat to dine there.

New Orleans is a fascinating city, but I was alone and lonely. I could not forget Tom though many months had passed. Christmas Eve, I invited Anne to share dinner with me because Bill was not due home until morning. Christmas Day, I telephoned everyone in my family. Then I got into my Studebaker and drove for miles along the Gulf

Coast Highway to Baton Rouge and almost to Mobile. It was better than sitting alone in my apartment.

In early January, I met a Navy Nurse from a nearby N.A.S. who wanted to vacation in Mexico. The idea appealed to me and we went to a travel agency and made reservations. We drove in my red Studebaker, spending one night in Houston and another night in San Antonio before crossing the Rio Grande into Mexico. That night we stayed at the Gran Hotel Ancira in Monterrey. We garaged the car there and flew to Mexico City.

At the airport, a statuesque Aztec guide met us with a limousine. We were driven to our hotel and given a packet detailing our tours and valuable information about shopping and restaurants. And, also warning us not to drink the water.

Two women from Seattle joined us the next morning. We had personal guided tours in an air-conditioned limousine – a luxurious way to travel.

We visited Chapultepec, the famous murals of Diego Rivera, and grand cathedrals where magnificent statues of saints wore crowns ablaze with pure gold and rubies and large pearl necklaces around their marble shoulders. Then I saw the poor ragged people with downcast eyes begging for pesos outside. I marveled at the contrast between their condition and the wealth inside the cathedrals.

We spent an entire day at the awesome Pyramids to the Sun Gods. I climbed the largest one halfway up, but the stone ledges were so narrow, its steps so steep, I gave up.

One day we asked our Aztec guide if he'd take us to the cockfights. He tried to dissuade us but we insisted and he escorted us to a barn outside the city. The cocks had knives attached to spurs on their feet. Two birds were placed into the arena pit. It quickly became bloody as they slashed at each other. Just awful seeing such carnage. We soon departed.

My roommate knew a Mexican man and his wife from her hometown in Louisiana and they invited us to their home for dinner. Another evening, they took us to an excellent restaurant and then to the Jai Alai games. Sunday, we bought tickets for the bullfights – an especially colorful and exciting event.

The matador was a graceful dancer inside the ring, his costume bedazzling in the afternoon sunlight. It was bloody. But the bulls were so huge and fierce, it bothered me not. When they were slain with a single thrust, I yelled "Ole!" with the rest of the crowd.

We took a three-day limousine trip to Pueblo, Cuernavaca, and Taxco; stopping at historic places along the way. I purchased a few choice items in the silver capital of Taxco.

A few days later, my roommate suffered a ruptured eardrum and could not fly. We turned in our return plane tickets and took a rundown bus back to Monterrey instead. It was a nightmarish trip. But I certainly could not desert her in her condition.

All in all, my Mexican adventures were great fun and I have no complaints.

Back in New Orleans, two Navy Nurses had reported for duty aboard the transport ships and my liaison duty was finished. The new orders that arrived for me were indeed different. I was to be nurse procurement officer for the Third Naval District with headquarters in New York City.

My friend Anne had a wonderful treat for me before I left – a ticket to one of the Krewe Balls during Mardis Gras. Every one, even the most spectacular ones, must present themselves in formal attire along with their special invitations at the Krewe Ball. The evening was a fitting end to my time in New Orleans.

I enjoyed my stay in the Deep South, but I had no reservations about moving forward.

10. AN IRISH TENOR'S VOICE

February 15, 1950, I drove my Studebaker through the Holland Tunnel and found my way to the Saint George Hotel in Brooklyn Heights. Ann, the nurse I was replacing, had reserved my room. Next morning, she and I caught the subway on the hotel's lowest level, arriving soon after at the Federal Building at 90 Church Street in lower Manhattan. The seven-minute ride was the first of many to come.

Ann introduced me around the office, reviewed her publicity files with me, and showed me the paperwork on applications. I had much to learn about my new job and the survival techniques of living in New York City.

She urged me to attend as many public functions in uniform as I could, in order to garner publicity to aid in the recruitment of prospective Navy Nurse candidates. I was not sure publicity was my strong point, but I would persist nonetheless.

My first week in Manhattan, there was a sports show at the Coliseum uptown. After work, Ann and I went there in our uniforms and posed for promotional stills beside a Navy recruiting booth. The next morning, our pictures were in the Daily News and the Journal American. A day later, Ann called the Navy garage and they sent a car and driver to take us through the icy streets to Patterson, New Jersey, for a talk show and visit to the local Navy recruiting station.

New York City is a bustling metropolis and it was quite a trying time for me grasping the pace, its sheer size. We visited hospitals in every borough, giving talks to nurses to stimulate their interest in a Navy Nurse career. After another week, Ann left and the job was all mine.

Since the Third Naval District included all of New York State, New Jersey, and Connecticut, I needed to make out of town trips. First thing I did was to arrange for a Navy driving test. Driving an official Navy car would mean no expense to me. At the Brooklyn dock area where I went for the test, there was only a large station wagon for me to drive. I didn't mind the starting, stopping, and parking. Didn't even mind the forward driving through the obstacle course. I did have a tough time backing through those orange cone impediments. After driving with the examiner, a rather talkative and kindly Petty Officer, through a few side streets, he passed me. I received my Navy driver's license.

I telephoned the American Nurse Assoication headquarters and went to lunch with a couple of their nurses. Then I joined the A.N.A., to help my career. Rennie, my flight nurse friend, worked at St. Albans Naval Hospital on Long Island. We met almost every week that winter. I got tickets to Broadway shows and she'd take the train to Manhattan, and we'd dine together before the curtain rose.

I have always enjoyed the culture of New York City.

Since I had no special someone in my life, I concentrated on furthering my career. I completed two officer correspondence courses and applied for college through the Navy's educational program. By St. Patrick's Day, I had decided that paying the garage bill at my hotel was much too expensive. I drove my precious Studebaker down to North Carolina and left it for my brother Jay to sell. It was such a fright driving in Manhattan and Brooklyn during the workweek. I did not use my car much on the weekends.

I found a nice efficiency apartment at 57 Montague Street in Brooklyn Heights, a few blocks from the Saint George. It was across from the Borough President's house and a little park and promenade on the edge of the Hudson River. There was 24-hour doorman service and visitors were announced via intercom. I felt safe. The view of Manhattan and the Wall Street area from my rooftop was terrific. I almost felt like a real New Yorker.

Rennie and I drove to Philadelphia one weekend in May. Several of our flight nurse pals were now on duty at the Navy hospital there. We laughed and talked and shared our memories. I did not know it when I left them, but that would be the last time I'd see them again, save for Rennie.

It took months for me to plan an out of town recruiting trip, but I was ready to attempt a week's visit to Connecticut the first week of June. The Navy car and gasoline credit card both worked fine. I went to Danbury, New Britain,

New Haven, and Hartford. I spoke on radio shows in each city, spending at least part of my day at the local recruiting office. I also kept my appointments to talk with senior nursing students – something I really enjoyed doing.

Anne and Bill from New Orleans were vacationing at the New Jersey shore. I invited them to New York and bought tickets for us to see my old Potomac River chum, Henry Fonda, in *Mister Roberts* on June 16th. Anne's friend, Eileen, worked in a sportswear office in the Garment Center on Seventh Avenue. We met there to shop before our lunch that day.

As I was trying on some playwear, a brash young salesman pulled the dressing room curtains aside and walked right in!

"How's the fit" he asked me.

"Just fine. Now shoo," I said.

"Name's Billy. What's yours?"

"Kay."

"Glad to make your acquaintance, Kay."

"I'm sure. Billy, is it? Would you mind closing the curtains on your way out?"

"Yeah, sure. No problem," he confidently answered me.

The impetuous nature of these Yankee men!

There were apparel buyers up from New Orleans, so we made plans to meet at their hotel after the play. Anne and Bill and I stopped at Gallagher's Steakhouse on 52nd Street for an after-the-theater dinner. Eileen and that intrusive young salesman from her sportswear office were waiting for us.

Billy pulled up a chair beside me. "I was on the USS New Jersey during the war," he said. And then he proceeded to tell me about his life as a sailor in the South Pacific. "Navy sent me to officer's candidate school at Holy Cross. Things would have worked out, who knows, I might have been a Lieutenant Commander like you." Then he suddenly reached over and pulled a sticky price tag from the sole of my brand new pumps.

Thought I'd die of embarrassment.

Anne and Bill left by train for New Jersey. Billy walked out of Gallagher's with Eileen and me. He placed his right pinkie finger and thumb to his lips and a quick, shrill whistle commanded a Checker cab to pull over to our curb. Billy opened the door and then followed me inside.

"Where to now?" he asked me.

When the telephone rang in my office the next day, I was interviewing two nurses. It was that sailor again! I gave him only cool responses because I was busy. But I knew he felt snubbed. My friend Fort once told me that some of the pilots thought me too impersonal. Fort said he'd told them if they really knew me, they would understand that I was a warm and caring person. I explained this to Billy.

"No problem. So, what do you say? We going out tonight or what?"

We went to the Roosevelt Hotel Grill for dinner and dancing. "Keep the glasses filled," he told the waiter when we sat down at the table. We danced to beautiful romantic music while Billy sang softly in my ear.

Oh, my. He is a handsome young man, and an excellent dancer – an Irish tenor's voice.

The hours flew by. Then Billy excused himself. "Be back in a minute."

I wait and I wait, still he does not return. I refuse another drink from our waiter. Where is he? Oh, there he is.

"I got involved watching the television fight in the lobby," he said. I did not buy his lame story. It would be many years before he told me that he had to wait in the lobby for a friend of his to arrive with enough cash to pay our check.

An impetuous Yankee indeed.

Now my time was fully occupied. Billy either met me after work in Manhattan or at my apartment in Brooklyn later in the evenings. We saw each other every day, went to lots of movies, and found interesting little places for intimate dinners. He was a native New Yorker who seemed well acquainted with almost every nightspot in the city. Billy was an avid movie enthusiast and sports fan. We saw the

Broadway musical *South Pacific* together, and oh how romantic the play was, with all those beautiful songs.

I took Billy with me to visit Nell, my good friend from Watts Hospital and the Navy, who now lived on Long Island with her husband Jack and their two children. When Rennie came into the city for a weekend visit, Billy organized a fun evening at the Village Gate.

We were in love with each other and we were already talking about marriage.

I scheduled a two-week recruiting trip into upstate New York for early July. I had several places lined-up to visit. My travels would put lots of miles on the Navy car. The department office released my publicity photograph and information fliers ahead of my arrivals. Before I reached my first stop in Newburgh, Billy had already called there and left a message. And that pattern of his continued. I was flattered and loved his attention. Oh how that salesman could talk on the telephone! His phone charm impressed the secretaries in the offices along my way.

Billy and I continued to talk about our marriage plans.

When I entered the Binghamton recruiting office, the chief recruiter met me with news that our recently retired Director of Navy Nurses, Captain Nellie Jane Dewitt, had been waiting for an hour to speak with me. This lovely woman lived nearby on the Susquehanna River and invited me to stay in her home. I had a few appointments to keep, but I promised to drive back for the weekend.

Captain Dewitt seemed happy to have me there. We had lots of good talks about our beloved Navy. I am sure she missed the activities and camaraderie. Serving in the United States Navy is an all-consuming, yet, wonderful way of life.

Before I left, Captain DeWitt and her niece, a young lawyer, suggested I meet them Tuesday afternoon at The Krebs, a famous restaurant on Lake Skaneateles, one of the Finger Lakes. It was perfect. And I have never eaten food so well prepared.

My trip seemed endless – Elmira, Syracuse, Ithaca, Canandaigua, Oneonta, and towns in between. The drives were longer than I'd imagined, and it was hard driving – sometimes I had to speed to keep my appointments.

I am unsure where I left on the day I returned to New York City, but it was far away. Looking at my map, I tried to figure out the shortest route downstate. I made a mistake that led me through the middle of the Catskill Mountains, on secondary roads with unbelievable hills and treacherous curves. Crossing the George Washington Bridge into upper Manhattan, I knew I couldn't hang on much longer. As soon as I drove off the bridge, I pulled over by a pay phone and called Billy to please come get me. I waited by the phone booth until he arrived by subway. He drove us back to the Navy garage in Brooklyn. I was exhausted and shaky.

While I had been away, Billy had moved into my apartment. It really was time to get our marriage plans settled. We rushed about getting blood tests and filing official documents. The marriage license clerk at City Hall asked for two dollars. Billy turned to me and said, "Come on, Kay, where's your dollar? This is a partnership, isn't it?"

We could not decide about the actual ceremony. I wanted to be married by a Protestant Minister – preferably a Presbyterian one. But my fiancé was Catholic. "Kay, I don't care one way or the other," he said. "But I've been talking to some friends of mine and they were telling me I shouldn't have a Protestant marriage ceremony. Let me put on my thinking cap and come up with something else."

Sunday, we went to Rockaway Beach to meet his mother. "Listen, Kay, do me a favor. I don't want any problems, so I'm just going to tell her we're already married. Go along with it, okay?"

I was not happy about the lie, but I agreed to go along with it.

Billy's mother did not appear to be thrilled with his joyous news, but she was warm and friendly to me.

The following evening Billy said, "I got a great idea. Friend of mine is a Jewish Justice of the Peace up in Monticello – a couple of hours upstate. Let me give him a call. We can ride up there tonight and get married."

And so that is what we did: An Irish Catholic Ex-Enlisted Man and a Southern Protestant Navy Officer married by a Jewish Justice of the Peace.

"Hey, Kay, figure it like this – we got all our bases covered."

The next morning at work, I showed my wedding ring to Rita my WAVE officer friend. She quickly spread the news and the office filled with noisy co-workers. My commanding officer delivered his best wishes and also gave me the rest of the day off. I telephoned my family and friends, shocking most of them. Rennie was the only person who had any inkling of my plans.

Life was a honeymoon for us even though we worked as usual. There were always new and interesting things to do and different places to visit in the city. Business at the Navy office had picked up because of the Korean War situation. I processed more applications and interviewed numbers of nurses. My telephone rang with calls from friends who had received orders returning them to flight status. I felt secure that I would remain in my present job if I continued to find lots of new nurses for the Navy. My husband was not so sure.

"We have to get you pregnant. Fast."

Two weeks after our marriage, my oldest brother Earl and his wife Sara Frances and their son William came to New York City on vacation, or perhaps it was to check on his little sister. I know not. I do know Earl felt responsible for our family after Dad's death.

I met them at the Taft Hotel on Seventh Avenue where they were staying. We took the subway back to Brooklyn and met Billy at Patricia Murphy's Candlelight Restaurant. After dinner we walked to our apartment. Then my husband took Earl and William to Ebbets Field for a Dodger game.

In the early autumn of 1950, one of the local television stations interviewed me on a program about women in the military hosted by Fanny Hurst, a well-known author. Rita and I represented the WAVES and Navy Nurses along with women from the Air Force, Army, and Marine Corps.

Billy told his friends they could meet his new wife by

watching their television sets. I doubt if my appearance received rave reviews – but each of us did try our best to pitch our talks toward recruitment for her particular branch of service.

I canceled my request for more college education – it was understood, a year of college paid for by the Navy, required a commitment for three more years. Now that I was married and planning a family, it just could not work.

Billy's friend in New Jersey operated a vending machine franchise for Sunshine Biscuits and business was evidently doing well. There was one franchise available in New York City and my husband wanted to purchase it. And so "The Partnership" invested. Next, we found a most attractive, newly built ranch style house with fieldstone front in Ardsley in Westchester County, only twenty miles north of Manhattan. The house was more expensive than we'd thought, but it was in a lovely area of town and it had real plaster walls and hardwood floors. We decided we wanted this house to be our home. Somehow we'd manage the payments with our G.I. mortgage and I could cash-in my bonds and G.I. insurance policy.

Now we had a real home.

December 1950, we moved into our suburban home and became commuters, driving together to Billy's office at 96th Street and Columbus Avenue. From there, I took the subway down to Worth Street – my headquarters had moved to larger offices at 346 Broadway. One morning in late December of 1950, I gave the oath of office to ten nurses, the largest group I had ever sworn-in at one time. A Navy photographer was there and we made the newspapers again.

I learned I was pregnant in January of 1951.

Billy and I were proud of ourselves and happy with the idea of a baby, but there was also a little apprehension about other aspects. I felt well and there were no serious health issues, but I also became very careful about how I treated myself because of the baby. The rush hour subway rides were too rough for comfort. I decided to drive to work. Parking was impossible, so I asked for and received the Navy placard:

ON OFFICIAL BUSINESS FOR THE U.S. NAVY

With the sign in my car window, I now parked right outside the building every day.

I wrote a personal letter to the Director of Navy Nurses in Washington, Captain Winnie Gibson, giving her my happy news and suggesting I might not be the right kind of image our Navy wished to project – what with my ever-expanding belly.

Three days later my replacement arrived. I acquainted her with my duties as chief procurement officer. After two weeks of orientation with her, I resigned my commission through official channels and I was released from the Navy on March 19, 1951.

Ten good years of my life.

But I had great expectations for a wonderful future as a suburban wife and mother.

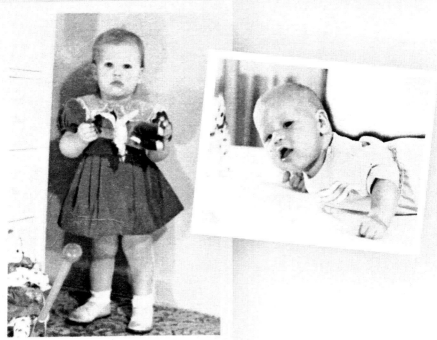

11. CONSTANT SOURCE OF JOY

Now that I was no longer a Navy career woman, I joined the local activities in Ardsley. A half-dozen neighborhood housewives met daily for coffee, and I happily became a member of the group. Most were almost my age; all had children ranging from toddlers to teenagers. The focus in Ardsley was on children and the educational affairs of the community.

My new friends came to my home to admire each new piece of furniture when it arrived. We were a diverse group of men and women from different sections of the county, including a rare native New Yorker such as Billy. Most of our neighbors were quite interesting people and I felt comfortable in their presence.

My youngest brother Paul, who had not yet met my husband, came to New York City on insurance business and spent a night with us in Ardsley. Billy and Paul had a great time together and I was happy because I always had a special fondness for my brothers. Later on, Jay brought his family up from Greensboro for a few days. For many years, I had spent time in their homes and it was my pleasure to host them now in mine.

Mother, too, was eager to check on my condition, so she and Mister Will came up by train for a visit. By this time, I was wearing maternity clothes but I still felt great. Billy drove us into Manhattan, stopping at the Cathedral of Saint John the Divine, Saint Patrick's Cathedral, and Rockefeller Center.

Driving into the Wall Street area, Mister Will saw the sign for the Trinity Church and he really came alive. For the first time, I learned that a great uncle of his had been an Episcopal priest at this historic church. The Wetmores, Mister Will's family, had moved from Connecticut down to North Carolina in the mid-nineteenth century. We looked about the church and found the name of Doctor James Wetmore prominently displayed on one plaque and in some of the church records.

Seeing his uncle's name thrilled my dear stepfather.

Three days later, I drove Mother and Mister Will up to Hyde Park where we toured Franklin Roosevelt's home. We also went to West Point that day. They said they had the trip of their lifetimes. Billy and I enjoyed having them because they were good company and they were so happy together.

Billy was busy from early morning until evening with his vending machine business. He did find time to shop for some needed baby furniture and brought home unpainted pieces – a crib, chest of drawers, playpen, a tiny table with a baby seat in the center, and matching straight-back chair. After placing the furniture in our basement where I'd be comfortable working, Billy brought me lead-free ivory paint, several brushes, and decals for decoration. I spent three weeks painting and applying decals to the baby furniture.

Billy carried the finished pieces upstairs to a room we had designated as the nursery. "Sweetheart, you did a great job. Maybe we should think about hiring you out," kidded my Irish New Yorker husband.

The last few weeks of my pregnancy were long and hot, and I felt so huge, and then the baby was several days past due. Billy called me from work and said, "Tonight we're going to that Chinese joint in White Plains. We'll have a couple daiquiris and maybe we'll perk-up the little rascal."

We did dine out that night, but it was I who perked-up along with labor pains about three in the morning. At a quarter to four in the afternoon on Saturday, September 8, 1951, I heard an infant cry. "Mrs. Baxter, you have a beautiful little girl," the doctor said, placing a perfect little baby on my abdomen. The birth had gone well and I was filled with a joy I could hardly wait to share with my husband. Billy assured me our daughter was really beautiful; and he looked quite proud and happy despite his ashen pallor.

A few days after Barbara's birth, I had a lovely surprise. My friend Lou from my flight nurse days walked into my hospital room. Lou was everyone's favorite friend, always so real, so natural. She promised to come to Ardsley on weekends whenever she could manage it.

I had my baby in the Navy Hospital because I'd been in the service when I became pregnant and my care would be excellent and just about free of charge. I wrote a check for five dollars and fifty-five cents to cover my officer's meals for the five days I spent there.

I feel sure Billy still has my canceled check somewhere in his file cabinets.

Barbara was truly the best of babies. Our first night at home I slept from eleven to five a.m. Unbelievable! I went in and out of her room all night to check on her respirations and her color.

Neighborhood mothers with preschool children asked me if their tots could come over to watch Barbara get her daily bath. So I made appointments for two sets of mothers and their offspring at a time. They found it fascinating to watch her and I was delighted to show off my daughter.

Lou came up frequently, and it was always a pleasure to be with her. Four months later, she received orders to the University of Colorado in Denver. I was sorry to say goodbye to yet another Navy Nurse friend.

Although Billy and I occasionally left Barbara for the evening, I now stayed home more. Life still so wonderful for us that before many months passed, I found myself pregnant again. We were surprised, that's a fact, but then we decided it would be best to have two children so near in age so they could be playmates. And for the second summer in a row, I wore only maternity clothes; but my health was excellent, Billy and I were in love, and Barbara was such a joy that we happily awaited our new baby.

Barbara took her first steps in late August of 1952 and I began to wean her off the bottle. I would soon have two children in diapers and both would require my assistance with food and drink. It would be easier if I got her off the bottle before she'd grab the new baby's.

Mother came to stay with me before I went to the hospital. She enjoyed playing with her granddaughter.

They talked together and Barbara's vocabulary increased.

I was completely awake when my baby was born on Friday, November 14, 1952. I heard a lusty cry and asked the doctor if I had a son. He replied, "You have a really handsome boy here."

Oh, my. He is just what I hoped for – another Billy. He is perfect like his sister. We are an All American Family: Man and Woman and Girl and Boy.

Billy Jr. was not quite six-weeks-old when we bundled up as a family, traveling to Billy's cousin, Rita McNamara's home in Merion, Pennsylvania, for Christmas dinner. Barbara sat on her new rocking horse all day, refusing to take her nap; but she was a good little girl and fell asleep holding onto her horse. Billy Jr. slept in his car bed. We adults had a wonderful visit and meal.

I was a busy mother. I had no household help and I didn't use a diaper service. I was so proud of my children. I loved caring for them. Billy Jr. had occasional bouts of night crying. Our family doctor found no chronic problems with him. We just decided that he loved being cuddled in the middle of the night. Their father loved to play with them when they were awake and dry, but he never changed a one of their dirty diapers even though I had two babies in that condition, at the same time!

Billy Sr. soon tired of the vending machine business. He took an insurance and real estate course and worked in a downtown office. We knew I needed to contribute financially, but I was not yet sure how to mange that. Two months later, Billy decided to open a ladies sportswear shop in the Village of Ardsley. He thought I could manage the store while he used his contacts in the Garment Center for the buying of merchandise.

I found Mrs. Tola, a capable and loving "mother substitute", to care for my nineteen-months-old daughter and my five-months-old son. I worked nine to five Monday thru Saturday at the clothing store. Neighbors dropped by to visit and shop. I felt happy to be working again.

Now I really had it all – a job and my loving family waiting for me at home.

That summer, a dear friend kept the children for a week, while my husband and I finally took our honeymoon trip, three years after our wedding. We did not entirely forget our two babies in the midst of romancing, but we did enjoy our extra freedom.

One day, I placed my babies in their playpen and read a book near them. Suddenly, Billy Jr. screamed. I looked up and he was lying on his stomach and Barbara was gleefully jumping up and down on his back. I quickly rescued him, thanking God he seemed all right.

The children needed a second playpen.

It was near impossible to even walk next door with my children. Barbara loved to walk, but especially she loved to skip away from me. Her brother had to be carried and Billy Jr. was a heavy little boy. I had a single stroller but could not manage to use it. However I tried one of them invariably had to be carried or held in a death-grip, leaving me no way to push the cart. But there were compensations. They were a constant source of joy to watch as they grew, responded to attention, and learned new things.

I marveled when Mrs. Tola, their sitter and friend, would hold one in each arm. She had raised twin girls who were now away at college. She was a dear lady my children adored, and an important part of our family.

Another family member was Cleo, our cocker spaniel. She loved to stay close to the playpens and keep the children entertained as she raced by them. Often I saw them holding toast through the bars to feed her. Other times they grabbed the food from her but Cleo never bit them.

One Saturday, Mrs. Tola called me at the shop to report Cleo was having puppies and that she needed help. Billy rushed home and delivered five adorable puppies. We made a spot in the basement for them until they were old enough for adoption.

Come to think of it, I wonder who the father of those puppies was?

12. MY PRIME CONSIDERATION

My husband was ten years younger than I. He had many single friends living in the city. Gary and Rudy and their girlfriends came to Ardsley with loads of toys for both children on Billy Jr.'s first birthday in November.

They also brought Piper Heidsieck champagne splits for the adults. As we drank, the children played around on the carpet. I glanced down and saw my one-year-old son finishing the last drop from a champagne glass and then reaching for another one. When I removed it from his hand, he cried out.

It was past their bedtime and they both began to wail. Gary reached for his camera, then my husband said, "Hold it a minute." He ran to the basement, returning with one puppy for each child. I quickly hung Christmas stockings from the fireplace mantel as Billy posed the kids with a puppy across each lap. It made a beautiful picture for our family Christmas cards of 1953.

I always carry a copy of that photograph in my wallet. A warm and wonderful feeling overtakes me when I look at their faces.

I was stunned when the real estate agent called and reported that we had a bona fide buyer for our house. It had been so long, I'd almost forgotten it was for sale. Billy was on a weekend trip, but when he returned home, we talked it over and decided to accept the offer.

Billy liked the country but he was a city man.

Now, several months prior to this weekend, he had fired me from our ladies sportswear shop. He'd started the argument, hoping I would resign. When I did not respond as angrily as his usual Irish friends might have, he had to fire me to get me out. Things at the store were surely in a financial mess. However, he was the one who took the cash receipts and kept the books. I am unsure just why we fell into arrears. Billy sold the store.

It was the right time to move.

On my son's second birthday in November of 1954,

we moved into a large two-bedroom apartment on the 16th floor of Fordham Hill in The Bronx. The rooms were large. There was cross-ventilation in the bedrooms and a spectacular view of the intersection where the Harlem and Hudson Rivers meet. Before we moved in, I had arranged that iron bars be bolted into each window, eight in all.

Safety for my children is my prime consideration.

Next thing I did, was cut the loops on the Venetian blind cords. I had read about a child strangling himself on just such a looped cord.

My husband stared down at the magnificently manicured green lawns outside our living room windows and said, "Look at this, Kay. Is this beautiful or what? And you know the best part? I don't have to do anything to keep it that way."

Billy was in his element again. I was confident I could become a real New Yorker. The children had a supervised playground with lots of wonderful equipment. We could take them to the park and to the zoo and to the beach. We will give Barbara and Billy every advantage of the rich cultural life of New York City.

From now on, I will feed my children early, settling them for the night, so their father and I can share intimate and romantic dinners again. I set our table with my best Madeira linen and my silverware from Taxco. We may eat by candlelight, the flame sparkling in our eyes. My heart is filled with love for my husband and my precious children. I am thankful for this happiness and for this wonderful world of ours. Bless us all, oh Lord.

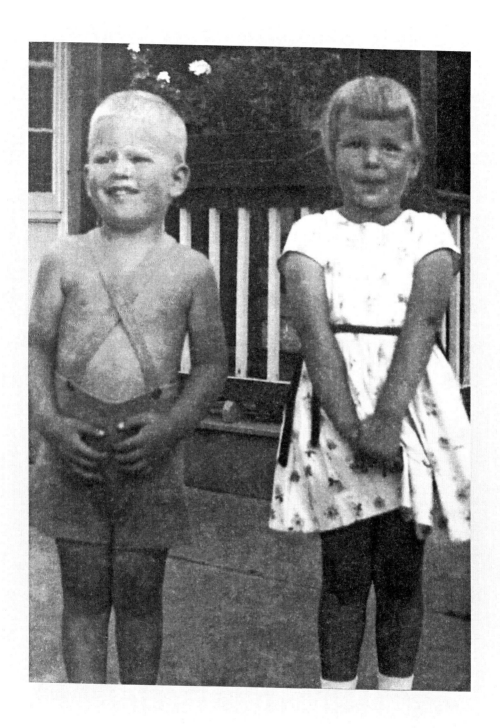

AFTERWORD

Dear Children,

The rest of the story, I leave for you to write. We had some great times before our family broke apart. There were difficult times, yet we survived them – without bitterness, I hope.

After I met and married your father, there was never another man in my life. I believed my marriage would last forever. For your sakes, I wish it would have endured, but it was not to be. No one is perfect, but I wanted so much for your lives to be happier. I am sorry I did not give you all you should have had; but I have loved you for every moment of your lives, and I have nurtured you the best I know how.

I am proud of you both. I am happy to have two lovely children who, though no longer adorable blonde toddlers, are, and will always be very, very special adults and essential to my happiness.

As I have looked back on my life, I realize that I have lived a wonderful life. There is some sadness, yet I feel no bitterness. My memories of the good moments have sustained me for years.

I am glad I have loved and have been loved, because it is absolutely essential to feel love.

My love is with you always.

Mom

The Rest Of The Story

On Sunday, January 10, 2010, Mom died at age ninety-four. Her last photograph was taken two months before her death. She was holding twins Leah and Jax Psaroudis, her six-week-old great-grandchildren. At that time, she was staying at a senior care center near my sister Barbara's home in northern New Jersey.

Shortly before then, my sister and her husband Mike had hosted Mom in their home, for the almost five years since she had left her assisted living accommodations at the Classic Residence Hyatt in Yonkers, New York. Her one-bedroom apartment there was on the 16th floor. She had spectacular view of the Hudson River and the sheer cliffs of the New Jersey Palisades.

I don't remember Mom happier than when she lived at the Hyatt from May 2002 thru December 2005. The enduring image I have of my mother is her sitting in her favorite chair reading a book. I don't know anyone who read more books than Mom. She read books every day and every night of her life – millions of words, descriptions, and dialogues.

Make Way For The Lady Ensign is the only book Kay Thompson Baxter ever wrote.

In April of 1991, twenty-five years ago, Mom was seventy-five years old and lived with her sister Mary Wood DiCostanzo in Chapel Hill, North Carolina. She asked me if I'd type her handwritten memoir.

"You can fix a sentence or two if you think it needs it," she said.

The original manuscript of *Make Way For The Lady Ensign* had no spelling, grammatical, or punctuation errors. There were no marks, erasures, or corrections of any kind on its pages. Her penmanship was precise and unmistakably feminine. After I transcribed it and had copies printed and bound, I mailed them to her.

Her friends and surviving family members read it and said how great they thought it was. Mom mailed her first copy to the Women in Military Service for America Memorial in Washington, D.C., along with her annual donation to help fund its construction.

On a visit with her in Chapel Hill in the spring of 1997, Mom said she wanted to tell me a story that she had purposely left out of her memoir. It was concerning her time working as a nurse at the Bethesda Naval Hospital outside Washington on the night of May 22, 1949. That spring night, the only patient on her ward was former Secretary of the Navy and the ex-first Secretary of Defense in United States history, James V. Forrestal. Mom explained that Secretary Forrestal was hospitalized at Bethesda after he had resigned and/or was forced out of the Truman administration.

"The scuttlebutt around the hospital," Mom said, "was that Secretary of Defense Forrestal had flipped-out at a cocktail party and he was running amuck and screaming, "The Russians are coming! The Russians are coming!"

"Did he act like that when he was on your ward? Was he nuts?" I asked her.

"I found Secretary Forrestal simply charming," she said. "We had such interesting conversations. Although he was quiet and reserved, he seemed to perk-up when I engaged him."

Mom explained that on that night, she'd told Forrestal she would bring her pocket-size cribbage board to work the next day so they could play. He smiled at her and responded he would like that very much. While leaving and standing inside the elevator, her patient, clad in his robe and pajamas, stood at attention outside his room. "Goodbye, Lieutenant Commander Thompson," said Forrestal, snapping-off his military salute. Mom saluted him back and said, "Goodnight, Mr. Secretary" just as the elevator doors closed.

The next morning, she heard the radio report that James V. Forrestal, the former Secretary of the Navy and America's first Secretary of Defense, was found dead on the third-floor roof below the 16th-floor kitchen window. The official Navy review board held an inquiry, my mother said, but they never called her to testify. Mom had heard that another Navy Nurse at Bethesda named Thompson (who she never met) did give some sort of testimony.

I was mind-blown.

Not only did I not know this story. I'd never even heard of James V. Forrestal or read or saw any news articles, books or documentaries about Forrestal's death. Mom said she told no one her story in almost fifty years.

"I just think that's one story you should know, Billy."

On July 25, 2000, my father flew down to North Carolina to surprise his ex-wife and celebrate their fiftieth wedding anniversary. By that date, they had been divorced for almost thirty years and separated for almost forty. But they had always remained close and involved in the lives of my sister and me.

Billy Sr. took her and Mary Wood to Durham to the Duke Inn on the university campus for dinner, cake, and champagne. The next day they drove to the Piedmont where her family farm had once operated and visited the Third Creek Church cemetery. Mom put flowers on the graves of her father John William Thompson and her mother Katherine Fleming Thompson.

It was not the last time our mother and father were together.

Less than a year later, my Aunt Woody called me and said she had found my mother in distress and that she was in the hospital. I flew down to Carolina and moved into Mom's basement apartment and visited her every day and night for a week. My sister Barbara, a R.N. like my mother, also flew down.

Mom was in and out of consciousness, her arms and legs flailing at times. She could barely mutter any words and did not seem to recognize anyone. The doctors were baffled and could make no determinative diagnosis about what was wrong with her. Barbara had to leave and go back to New Jersey for work and to take care of her family. I stayed.

Her doctor told me again that there was no definitive explanation for what was wrong with her. He thought it might be some form of encephalitis but the tests were inconclusive. "Your mother is dying," he told me. "There's nothing more we can do for her. You have to take her to a hospice."

I rode in the back of the ambulance with her twelve miles up the road to Hillsborough. The hospice was situated out in the country. Mom was given a room with huge sliding glass doors overlooking a meadow and pond where cows and horses grazed. My cousin Gloria and my cousin Joe Jr. came over and we read her stories from *Make Way For The Lady Ensign*. But she just continued to moan and chatter gibberish and show no real response.

One week later, I gave my permission to discontinue her IV medicine and nourishment. That night, after they removed the medical equipment, I moved her bed to face the sliding glass doors. I adjusted her bed-head, and then I turned off the lights so she might somehow see the idyllic, moonlit scene.

I sat in a chair holding her hand and wept.

Around ten o'clock, a very tall grey-haired man in a black suit knocked on the door and stuck his head inside. "Do you mind if I pray with your mother?"

"Sure, please do."

I didn't ask him what his story was. I figured he was a local preacher doing his rounds at the hospice. He pulled up a chair on the opposite side of the bed and held her other hand. And then he recited Psalm 23: "...Yea, though I walk through the valley of the shadow of death, I will fear no evil..." When he ended it with "Amen," Mom said, "Thank you."

That was the first logical response my mother spoke in almost two weeks.

"Your mother is going to be fine."

I thanked the Man. He left and shut the door.

Midnight, I kissed her goodbye and went back to Chapel Hill. I figured she would probably die that night.

When I arrived at the hospice the next morning, the nurse on duty said something had happened to my mother. "Is she dead?" I said.

"Go in and look for yourself."

Mom was sitting up in bed eating from a cup of yogurt. She smiled at me and said, "Billy, just how long have I been here?"

Whatever ailment possessed her was now gone. She had no remembrance of the past two weeks. The doctors never did know why she was sick in the first place or why she was now completely healed and in her right mind. Within hours, the administration told me that since Mom wasn't dying anymore they had to release her from the hospice.

"Your mother is the first and only patient to ever leave this hospice alive," the Nurse told me.

I found her a rehab/nursing home in Durham. She stayed there for thirty days until her Medicare cut-off on

Friday, April 13, 2001. Meantime, I went back to New York City, and my sister and I found an assisted living facility on Riverdale Avenue in The Bronx. We moved up her belongings and furniture. Mom became a New Yorker again.

At eighty-six, she met Jack Marchand and they became friends and dining companions. Jack drew maps for the Army during World War II. After the war, he became the art director and main illustrator at LOOK Magazine. Mom and Jack became so fond of one another, they both decided to leave their assisted living building in The Bronx. They moved a mile up Riverdale Avenue to the more luxurious and the not-too-much-more expensive Hyatt Classic Residence on the Yonkers borderline. My father took the bus from midtown Manhattan nearly every week to visit with her... and Jack.

Mom cherished the attention of both men.

When her savings account was drained after four years she moved in with my sister and her family in New Jersey. Jack died a few months later. On August 8, 2005, my father hosted a dinner at Kennedy's Restaurant on West 57th Street in Manhattan to celebrate Mom's ninetieth birthday.

January of 2010, Mom was at Saint Claire's Hospital in Sussex, New Jersey, where my sister Barbara was a nurse. Her room was directly across from the nurses' station, where her daughter and the other nurses could watch over her. The last time I visited my mother, her eyes were closed and she had a serene look on her face. I knew she heard me. And she knew she was loved.

Mom left us at the age of ninety-four.

Kay Thompson Baxter lived nine more years after she left the North Carolina hospice. She outlived her brothers and her beloved Mary Wood. And she lived long enough to hold her great-grandchildren in her arms.

She was cremated according to her wishes. We buried her ashes in the Thompson family plot at the Third Creek Church cemetery. The Reverend William E. Thompson, a Presbyterian minister and her brother Earl's son, said the words.

Jack Baxter
April 30, 2016